"Mario Cartaya's "Journey Bac[...] Childhood Footprints" is a love s[...] States). What a superb storyteller. This is a beautiful, meaningful story. Indeed, it is a treasure."

David Lawrence Jr.

Author of *A Dedicated Life: Journalism, Justice and a Chance for Every Child*; Retired publisher—Miami Herald; Chair of The Children's Movement of Florida

"On this bittersweet journey of rediscovery, Mario Cartaya finds little-remembered places of his pre-revolutionary childhood, family he never knew he had, and a Cuba that is bewitching but still captive to the failed economic and political system that triggered the diaspora long ago. His story packs an emotional wallop."

David Powell

Author of *Ninety Miles and a Lifetime Away: Memories of Early Cuban Exiles*

"This true story is a love story as heartfelt as any told in a novel. A tale of love of family, place, and relationships.
"It will trigger memories of one's own childhood experiences and bring back those happy and/or trying times; but if lost, may suggest you journey to your own vault wherever it may be."

Charles Redner

Author of *Long-A-Coming; Down But Never Out; Terror Travels the Devil's Highway*; Executive Editor and Publisher—The Hummingbird Review

"Mr. Cartaya has a crisp, colorful and descriptive writing style. His moving passages tap into the readers' sentiments and enable them to feel the many emotions and astonishing surprises the author experienced during his first return to Cuba—after five decades of exile in the United States. His story conveys a spiritual message often lost in these materialistic times: When we engage on a voyage of self-discovery, as the author did, the Universe often supplies surprising guideposts that point us in the right direction."

Kingsley Guy

Author of *Piercing the Veil: A Skeptic Journalist Discovers Unseen Worlds* and *Queen of Heavens*; Retired journalist who served 23 years as the editorial page editor of South Florida's Sun-Sentinel newspaper

JOURNEY BACK INTO THE VAULT

In Search of My Faded
Cuban Childhood Footprints

MARIO CARTAYA

To order additional copies of this book, contact:
Xlibris
844-714-8691
www.Xlibris.com
Orders@Xlibris.com
834089

CONTENTS

The people and events depicted in this book are real.

Dedicated to My Father
Juan Ignacio Cartaya

(Circa 1952) My mother, me, older brother and father

The turbulent winds of change swept over Cuba in 1959, leaving my father with little choice but to make the heart-wrenching decision to flee the land of our birth with my mother, brother, and me toward a new life in the United States.

Life as a political exile was challenging for my father. Nonetheless, he wore the responsibility of providing for us with steadfastness, humility, a healthy sense of humor, and an uncompromising optimism that a better future was always within reach.

My father taught us, by example, how to believe in ourselves, dream, work hard, overcome adversities and strive to become the authors of our individual stories. He was our unwavering catalyst of hope – our rock. He often worked two to three jobs at a time, unselfishly using disposable income to help family members still in Cuba join us in the United States; noble acts he often described as his penance for having separated us from the loved ones we once left behind.

In time, through hard work, grit, and determination, he lifted us from immigrant want into a life no different than our middle-class American neighbors.

My father unfortunately died while still young and was buried with much unresolved pain and anguish. It has always saddened me how his life, uprooted by unforeseen challenges and geopolitical events he had no control over or interest in, denied the dreams and once-promising future of a good man.

Long ago, I dedicated my life to be a validation of his decisions, principles, integrity, and unconditional love. I have always sought to honor him.

He was my father and best friend.

This story is dedicated to his memory.

PREFACE

The Vault

An Unanticipated Reality

Have you ever returned to that place where you keep the painful and inconvenient memories you chose to discard along the way?

The evolution of our individual uniqueness weaves through our life experiences in unpredictable paths as we mature. It is a normal and transforming process by which increasingly sophisticated forms of individuality develop from an initial sense of identity and self-concept. As we bond with our family and conform to society's culture, mores, traditions, language, and expectations, we abandon our previous identities and store them, along with other experiences we seek to forget, inside a protective subconscious place we rarely choose to acknowledge or visit.

If your path through individualization, however, is usurped by an event so powerful that it changes the trajectory of your life, thrusting you into a new reality where the truths you once built your life upon no longer apply, then what becomes of you?

If at an age when socialization and acceptance are a priority but your uniqueness is interpreted by others as nonconforming, how do you rebuild your identity in order to assimilate?

I know the answers all too well.

Leaving My Promised Life

The first nine years of my life were spent in Cuba, the country of my birth, where I developed my earliest sense of identity, self-concept, and personal uniqueness. Being the youngest son of a middle-class family and having grown to love baseball, the arts, and attending school, I thought of myself as smart and social with youthful impulses that often got me into trouble. I enjoyed the support of my extended family core and shared their expectation that, like them, I would eventually create a successful life in Havana and continue to grow our family bonds there.

It wasn't meant to be. On November 13, 1960, my parents, brother, and I fled Cuba and immigrated toward an unanticipated future in the United States, leaving behind our heritage, possessions, loved ones, the lives we built, and the futures we planned. The next day I awoke in Miami, a stranger in a strange land, confused and uncertain about my new American reality. At the tender age of nine, incapable of understanding the challenges I would face during an alternate life in exile, I grew wary of my suddenly undefined future and the collection of choices I would have to make in order to forge a new American persona.

During the weeks and months that followed, I developed insecurities I had never known. At an age when peer acceptance is so important, I was often treated by my classmates and teachers as *different*. Sometimes I felt invisible to those too busy to bother with a young foreigner they did not care to understand. My confidence suffered, and I started to question who I was.

I dreamed of the day I would be accepted by my fourth-grade classmates, teachers, and neighborhood kids.

"The self is not something ready-made, but something in continuous formation through choice of action."
—John Dewey

Eventually, I started to speak enough English to communicate; experienced core American traditions like Halloween, Thanksgiving, and the Fourth of July; discovered hot dogs, hamburgers, and apple pie; and learned to recite the Pledge of Allegiance. Soon, I was even singing every word of the American national anthem. Most importantly, my athleticism helped me excel in football and baseball, allowing me to be picked in the early rounds of sandlot games and rewarding me with the peer acceptance and recognition I sought most.

Almost a year after my arrival in the United States, the process of acceptance, socialization, and assimilation had begun.

I was no longer invisible.

Finally, the day arrived when I adjusted to my new culture and felt no different than my American-born friends. After all, the United States was the land of cowboys, Superman, Mighty Mouse, and rock and roll. It was home to Major League Baseball, and with a little luck, I could watch Mickey Mantle, Willie Mays, and Sandy Koufax on *Game of the Week* telecasts.

Loving my new country was easy; becoming an American took a little time.

A Silent Consequence

The process of metamorphosis into an American taught me how to methodically store my inconsequential Cuban identity, increasingly irrelevant Cuban childhood memories, the struggles of my early years in exile, the agony of our family's separation, and the suffering associated with the eventual deaths of each of the loved ones I once left behind in Cuba—never to see again— inside a protective subconscious vault of my own creation.

During my formative early teens and against the background noise of the turbulent 1960s, I sought out positive role models to emulate while meticulously crafting my new American self. It was a period of great exploration and constant change. My high school years were influenced by a handful of educators and baseball coaches who believed in me and steered my efforts toward the pursuit of my dreams and goals. In college, I had mentors who helped me fulfill my educational journey, Hispanic peers who, like me, had embarked on similar voyages of transformation, and American-born roommates who taught me how to think, act, and live as an American. Today, those educators, mentors, peers, and roommates still live within me and form a major part of who I became.

By the time I graduated from the University of Florida, I had become an American architect—confident in my new persona and hopeful for the future. Proud of my achievements and eager to continue exploring my American dream, I lost all awareness of the protective subconscious vault I once built.

There was no longer a need for my protective subconscious vault.

Four decades later, having reached security in most aspects of my life and watching my grown American children marry and have American children of their own, I started to question who I was and how I had arrived at this juncture in my life. Missing the memories, identity, humanity, and sentiments from my Cuban childhood, I grew increasingly aware of the vault inside me once more.

Instinctively, I knew that the time had finally arrived for me to breach the protective walls of my subconscious vault and reclaim my Cuban past. Then, and only then, would I learn the totality of who I was, not just who I had become.

EXILE AND RETURN: FINDING CLARITY

The Morning that Changed My Life

Every story has a beginning and this one starts during the early dawn hours of January 1, 1959. Already awakened by the sounds of blowing horns, loud voices, and music playing outside my house, I watched as my grandfather reached inside the mosquito net draped over my bed, lifted me into the air, and hugged me amid all the noise outside the protective walls of my second-floor bedroom.

"Mayito," I remember my grandfather jubilantly saying that day, "today marks the end of Batista's regime and the return of democracy to Cuba. Hug me. This is a day we will never forget."

Only seven years old and half asleep, I had no idea what he was talking about. I stared at him, not really happy to have been awakened so early in the morning, and wondered what all the fuss outside my house was about.

Amid all the confusion that fateful New Year's Day, my grandfather and I never imagined just how much our lives were about to change.

During the months that followed, Fidel Castro consolidated his power in Cuba, shunned democratic elections, and orchestrated the installation of a cruel and totalitarian regime throughout the island. He branded himself an antagonist of the United States and courted the Soviet Union for economic assistance and military protection—acts that forever changed the trajectory of our family's future.

Starting in late 1959, Cuba's new revolutionary government embarked on a campaign to document and nationalize American properties and businesses throughout Cuba. My father, Ignacio, owned a business specializing in accounting and retail sales of American-made Frigidaire and Sylvania products. His clients' records—including the locations and value of all investments, retail stores, maintenance shops, storage facilities, and merchandise inventory throughout the island—were meticulously kept in his company's business ledgers.

The government's nationalization efforts eventually found my father at his business address. One fateful morning in 1960, two machine gun-carrying militia personnel barged into his office looking for the company's ledgers.

It did not go well for my father.

With the machine gun-toting rebels aggressively walking around his office, yelling threats, and demanding his records, my father faced his worst fears as he weighed their abusive personal attacks, unlawful demands, and rapidly escalating challenges to his business against the need to survive the day. In the end, his righteousness prevailed. He refused to give them anything.

My dad's defiance of the government transgressors' demands that day, however, culminated in an argument that ultimately led to his detention.

During his confinement, my father was escorted to a meeting with Cuban revolutionary officials for an interrogation that quickly turned into accusations, lectures, and threats until finally concluding with an order to surrender his business ledgers before the end of the day. With no judicial request supporting their demands, he bravely refused again.

Furious with his perceived insubordination, the lead interrogator, Revolutionary Commander Che Guevara, aggressively approached my father and proceeded to berate and threaten him in a brutal and sustained tirade of anger.

Life was cheap during the early days of the Cuban Revolution. My dad's defiance of Cuban military authority that day had placed his life in real and imminent danger. A lieutenant, friends with my father since childhood, intervened and convinced Commander Guevara that he would personally ensure my father complied with their demands.

Fortunately, my father eventually handed over his ledgers and the rebels backed down. Unfortunately, he was now blacklisted by Castro's revolutionary regime and warned that his future safety in Cuba was no longer guaranteed.

That day my dad's life was mercifully spared; but his fate, as well as ours, was sealed. My father, mother, brother, and I would have to leave Cuba.

A few days later, peeking through our home's second-floor balcony balusters, I watched my father ask our extended family members gathered in the living room below for permission to leave Cuba with my mother, brother, and me toward a new life of exile in the United States. Everyone in the living room groaned and started to cry. Sitting alone on the second-floor balcony above them, I wept as well. It was a dramatic and life-changing moment for all of us.

I did not know what to expect—I am not sure if my parents or the rest of my family did either. After all, who can predict an unplanned alternate life in an unknown land?

In the coming months, my father sold his business to his partner and traveled to Miami in an effort to secure employment. By September 1960, everything was arranged and we prepared to leave. Just one thing, however, remained to be done.

Before our planned departure in November, my father wanted us to simultaneously discover and say goodbye to the land of our birth. One cloudless Cuban morning, my parents, brother, and I slid into our blue-and-white 1957 Ford sedan and drove off on a farewell tour of Cuba toward Viñales Valley in the west before continuing on to Santiago de Cuba in the east—stopping at several coastal villages, hamlets, and historical towns along the way. Once we reached Santiago, my family and I attended mass at Cuba's holiest shrine, *La Basilica del Cobre*, and prayed for the Virgin of Charity to protect us during our exile and care for the loved ones in Cuba we were soon to leave behind.

A few weeks after our Cuban farewell trip, on November 13, 1960, my father, mother, brother, and I prepared to leave our home in Havana for the short drive to José Martí International Airport. Later that day, we would be climbing the mobile metal steps leading to our seats inside the cabin of a Pan American Airways flight to Miami.

My grandmother, succumbed by an unimaginable and uncontrollable grief, locked herself in her bedroom. My grandfather put on a brave face and mustered a smile as he hugged and kissed us goodbye. My uncle Miguel drove us to the airport. We never saw one another again.

Becoming an Exile

Once airborne, the sounds of the airplane's engines continuously marked the passage of time and distance away from our home and the loved ones we were leaving behind—every rotation of the propeller blades bringing us closer to an uncertain future in a new land. Inside the cabin, everything was eerily quiet except for the intermittent sobbing from some of the passengers.

In an effort to dull the grief and sorrow surrounding me on the airplane that morning, I replaced the reality of our exodus with a playful image of my little red Erector toy crane gently lifting me into the beautiful, cloudless blue skies of the Florida Straits. It was a replacement reality I hoped would bring me to an American winter wonderland I had only seen on television.

Forty-five minutes after departing from Havana, we arrived in Miami—numb, but unbroken. Fortunately, my mother, father, brother, and I were together. Unfortunately, there was no snow in Miami to greet me that day.

That day, I woke up in Havana as a Cuban national; by nightfall, I slept in Miami as an exile in a strange land.

The Vault

During the 1960s there was little, if any, communication with Cuba. It was an era defined by the failed Bay of Pigs invasion, numerous ill-conceived and executed American attempts to assassinate Fidel Castro, and the nearly apocalyptic Cuban Missile Crisis. As a result, travel to the island was prohibited, telephone access became impossibly restricted, and mail service was unreliable. By the time President Kennedy's administration negotiated an end to the Cuban Missile Crisis and enacted a policy of maximum pressure on Cuba's now Marxist-Leninist government, most forms of communication with Cuba stopped.

Our American exile had become permanent.

My maternal grandparents, Marcos and Isaura; Uncle Miguel; and Aunt Ileana became terminally ill in Cuba during that time. Unable to travel there during their final days, my parents, brother, and I searched for ways to stay in contact with them. Without reliable telephone service or mail delivery, our only form of communication became frustratingly limited to short and often-encrypted telegraphs. Never had our family's separation seemed so great or the distance between us so far.

By 1968, they were all gone. We never saw them again. None of us ever got to say goodbye.

I buried the suffering caused by the deaths of my loved ones in Cuba, including the feelings of guilt and impotence associated with our inability to see them during their time of need, inside the same protective subconscious vault I had already built to shelter me from the pain of my now irrelevant Cuban identity, fading childhood memories, and struggles from my first years in exile.

My vault worked well. In time, I stopped feeling its presence or contents inside me.

The Siren Song

Now in my adult years, I felt an innate need to breech my subconscious vault in search of the Cuban identity and childhood memories I once discarded to a life of obscurity inside its protective walls. I did not know what I would find there. I did not know the effect it would have on my life. I just knew I had to try.

I had reached a point in my life where I needed to make peace with myself, conquer the unknown demons lurking within me, find the missing pages of my Cuban story, recover a lifetime of lost memories, and achieve those closures long denied. Instinctively, I knew I would have to travel to Cuba and walk on the faded footprints of my childhood steps in order to succeed.

A siren song had awakened deep within me and was calling me back to the land of my birth.

It was time to return to Cuba.

Going back to Cuba would not be easy for me. My first attempt, in 2003, was on a People to People Ambassador Program hosted by the Urban Land Institute. For reasons I might never know, my Cuban visa was never granted, leaving me with little alternative but to watch from afar as the group left without me. Once President Obama was elected and enacted a new US-Cuba policy of rapprochement, I decided to try again. This time I obtained the Cuban visa, bought my charter flight tickets, and reserved a hotel room in Havana. A week before my scheduled August 2012 departure, however, I was diagnosed with non-Hodgkin's lymphoma. Facing an unanticipated health crisis, I canceled my plans and concentrated on restoring my health and well-being. I made the right decision; the treatments worked well, and additional tests showed I was in complete remission.

During my recovery, however, I often wondered if the effort and stress of trying to visit Cuba were worth it. I grew confused and waited for clarity.

Clarity and Courage

When President Obama traveled to Cuba on March 21, 2016, my son and I watched his much-anticipated address to the Cuban government and people on my home television screen. We held our breath as the American president climbed onto the stage at the *Gran Teatro de la Habana*, steeled his look, and started a speech of hope and reconciliation, five decades in the making, by proclaiming, "*Cultivo una rosa blanca.*" (I nurture a white rose)

President Obama's preamble to the most significant speech ever delivered by an American president on Cuban soil had just quoted the words of redemption, peace and forgiveness written by Cuban poet and patriot José Martí during Cuba's War of Independence from Spain. Our president's acknowledgment of Martí's humane and historical offering of friendship to friends and adversaries alike, promised to end five decades of Cuban-American hostilities, replacing it instead with a new era of reconciliation.

A day I often feared might never arrive had finally dawned, shining its bright light of hope upon all those with peace, love and goodwill in their hearts.

President Obama, however, did not travel to Havana just to bury the last remnants of the cold war; he had come prepared to plant the seeds of change in the island as well. His speech, delivered with Cuba's leaders in attendance and televised on both sides of the Florida Straits, touched the hearts and minds of Cubans and Americans everywhere. He released the *American promise and dream* onto the Cuban consciousness that day and served it flawlessly to a stunned auditorium audience and spellbound Cuban nation.

The American president spoke eloquently and honestly for all of us. My son and I applauded his courage, bonded in the enormity of the moment, and grew inspired for the future of the country I now desperately felt the need to rediscover. Obama's confidence, bravery, and determination that day energized and motivated me.

I regained the resolve to acknowledge the siren song within me and decided, once again, to follow it wherever it led in search of my forgotten Cuban past.

I had found the clarity I needed.

On November 13, 1960, a young boy, scared and nervous, was playfully lifted by an imaginary little red toy crane from his Havana living room and gently dropped off in Miami. On May 16, 2016, a grown man in need of repairing the torn and frayed tapestry of his life, longing to find the images of his early childhood and hopeful of bonding with the people and land he once fled, finally returned to the country of his forgotten youth.

This is the story of the incredible and extraordinary events that awaited me and would unfold during my return journey to Cuba. It is an existential tale of retracing the footprints of your childhood steps, facing your past, achieving closures denied, and finding the inner peace, redemption, and forgiveness necessary to reach the clarity of mind and purity of heart required to discover the true meaning and essence of your life.

DAY 1

SAYING HELLO

A Longing to Know

On May 16, 2016, I arrived at Miami International Airport looking to board the early flight to Havana. Barely four o'clock in the morning, dozens of passengers were already in line for processing at the American Airlines check-in counter. Most were Cuban Americans returning home to visit family members; others were simply going there for a good time.

Fifty-six years after leaving Cuba, I was finally returning to the land of my birth in search of my childhood memories.

I settled at the rear of the line and waited for my turn to check in with the airline official. There was hope and wonder around me that morning—everywhere I looked, people were smiling.

Some of the passengers were carrying inordinate quantities of suitcases and assorted bags with them. Others were taking small air conditioners, undercounter refrigerators, and television sets. Most were bringing much needed clothing, medicines and daily necessities—not readily found in Cuba today—for their loved ones back home.

A grandfatherly looking man, traveling alone, was carrying a rather large and cuddly teddy bear—it made me smile. Some young boy or girl in Havana was about to be very happy once he cleared Cuban Customs later this morning.

After checking in the one small bag I was bringing, my wife, Pam, and I headed toward the TSA security checkpoint knowing full well that once we got there I would be continuing on my journey alone. My trip to Cuba would not include her. I could not totally open myself to the raw emotions I was certain to face during my journey of self-discovery if I simultaneously felt the need to shelter her from my pain.

We walked in silence—our emotions expressed only by the tight grasp of our hands.

Once we reached the queue for TSA security, it was time for us to say goodbye. Careful not to show any unintended emotions that might cause my wife distress, I raised the wall I often use to mask my feelings and gently assured her, "Baby, don't worry about me. I'll be fine."

She stared at me in silence and mustered a feigned smile as tears swelled from her sad green eyes onto her cheeks.

"Please don't cry," I said, "I will only be gone a week."

"I am not crying because you are leaving," she responded.

"Well then, why are you crying?" I asked.

"Because I know you are finally going to find the answers you've always needed," she said. "I'm only happy for you."

She understood.

"Smile, You Are in Cuba"

The flight from Miami to Havana was short and uneventful. Engulfed within an eerie state of calm and filled with countless dissimilar emotions, I dulled my surroundings and kept to myself. Less than forty-five minutes after leaving Miami, we were flying over Havana's northern coastline.

I looked out the airplane's window and saw the land of my birth once more.

A few minutes later, our chartered aircraft landed at Havana's José Martí International Airport and roared down the arrivals runway until ironically coming to a complete stop just outside the same, seemingly unchanged, airport terminal building from where my father, mother, brother, and I once fled Cuba amid much pain and confusion.

I had come full circle.

I sat frozen in my passenger seat waiting for the aircraft's door to open and thought about the life-changing events that led to my parents' decision to flee our homeland, the sad goodbyes with family members on the day we left, the chaos defining our last hours in Havana inside the same terminal I was about the re-enter, and the anticipation I felt as a nine-year-old boy to fly on an airplane for the first time.

Most of all, however, I thought about how—after all these years and two previous failed attempts to return—I was finally back in Cuba, anxious to start the search for my long forgotten Cuban childhood memories.

Once the aircraft's doors finally opened, I exited the cabin and climbed down the airport's mobile ladder ever so slowly, never taking my eyes off the tarmac on Cuban soil below. I reached the last step, looked curiously at the first sights of Cuba around me, and spiritedly stepped on Cuban soil once more.

Not wanting to give in to the overwhelming emotions suddenly pouring over me, I dulled my senses again and convinced myself I was fine.

I followed the other passengers toward the terminal I had always associated with so many disturbing memories from my family's last day in Cuba and walked through its ancient exterior doors directly into the Cuban Customs holding room. Once inside, I hurriedly joined the rear of one of the several tidy international passenger arrival queue lines already formed and prepared to meet with one of the once-feared olive-green-uniformed Customs officials.

Alone and lost within my many emotions, I looked around the interior of my once dreaded terminal and realized that the place synonymous with my family's painful departure from Cuba fifty-six years ago, now surprisingly represented a welcoming portal into what promised to be a homecoming week of reconciliation, discoveries, and closure.

Today, the anguish of my last day in Cuba had incredibly given way to the hopes and wonder of a returning son.

The quiet and orderly Cuban Customs holding room at José Martí International Airport was a pleasant and calming surprise this morning. Everyone around me stood unusually still, moving only to make eye contact with the others in queue. No one spoke or even coughed—all stress and anticipation channeled into a most unusual silence belying the many long queue lines already formed.

The walls of the spartan holding room were bare except for a photograph of Raúl Castro and an official-looking government poster depicting a female military officer holding her index finger in front of her lips with a sign printed in large capital letters below her image that read "DO NOT RAISE YOUR VOICE." It was my first experience with Cuban crowd control—the uncomfortable silence in the room proved it was working.

Suddenly, it was my turn to meet a most unexpected and welcoming olive-green-uniformed female customs agent. Noticing my hesitant and quiet demeanor, she sighed and demurely asked me to stare into the security camera. I complied with what must have appeared to be an awkward expression.

"Smile," the pretty customs agent said, "you are in Cuba."

I told myself I was fine and smiled. She smiled back.

I thanked the female customs agent and walked slowly into the large adjoining room to retrieve my suitcase.

The ancient 1950s baggage return room in José Martí International Airport still had its vintage baggage carousel winding interminably in and out of the wall separating the passenger baggage pickup area from the secured airside baggage unloading room beyond. Its walls were also bare except for the now-familiar Raúl Castro photograph and the faded poster of the military woman asking for silence.

I claimed my bag with the blue ribbon and baseball tag I always use when I travel and excitedly proceeded toward the arrivals terminal's exit doors—Cuba waited for me beyond them.

Soon, I would start searching for the faded childhood steps from my Cuban past.

One of Many Returning Sons

Once outside, the silence of the customs holding room and baggage area gave way to scores of Cubans screaming, cheering, and hugging their loved ones returning from abroad. Unfortunately, no one from my family was waiting for me here today—none of them had lived long enough to welcome me back. I took a soul-cleansing breath, thought about how different things could have been, and paused a moment to watch and enjoy the countless joyous reunions taking place around me.

Among all the noise, expressions of love, and carefree laughter, I spotted a little girl in a pink dress running toward the grandfatherly man I first noticed in Miami International Airport—still carrying the large teddy bear he brought with him.

Once the little girl reached him, she jumped into his arms, hugged him, and joyfully screamed, "*Abuelito!*" (Grandfather)

"*Mi amor*," responded the old man, his eyes tearing with emotion, "this teddy bear needs a new friend."

They hugged and kissed each other on the cheeks. She grabbed the teddy bear from her *abuelito*'s outstretched arms and held it tight against her chest. The grandfather, teddy bear, and little girl had found one another.

Lost amid the emotions of these beautiful family reunions, I realized that even though I was standing on Cuban soil for the first time in fifty-six years, all I felt was a most remarkable and welcomed sense of calm. I started looking into the crowd for Maidel (the young Cuban entrepreneur who was meeting me at the airport's arrivals area this morning and would serve as my driver all week), expecting him to identify himself by holding a sign with my name printed on it—to no avail. Finally, after asking several travel company representatives if they knew my driver, a tour-uniformed agent pointed him out.

Maidel walked toward me, introduced himself, and asked me to wait a couple of minutes while he ran into the adjoining parking lot to retrieve his car. A few minutes later, he pulled up to the arrivals curb in a brand-new black Chinese Geely sedan with very dark-tinted automatic windows. In a country where vintage cars from the 1950s and an assortment of comical homemade methods of transportation are the norm, the sight of this modern and very official-looking black sedan was something I did not expect.

I placed my lone bag inside the car's trunk and slid into the passenger's seat. Moments later Maidel and I were on our way toward the Hotel Nacional de Cuba, my home away from home while in Havana this week.

"With a Little Help from My Friends"
—The Beatles

José and George are two of my closest friends from South Florida. When they heard of my plans to travel to Cuba alone, they informed me that they would not allow me to go there without them. Their reasons for visiting Cuba, however, were different from mine.

My friends bring the party with them everywhere they go, and this time they wanted to take it to Havana. During dinner in Fort Lauderdale a couple of weeks later, the three of us agreed that during the day, they would accompany me to all those places I needed to visit on my sure-to-be emotional voyage of self-discovery. At night, however, I would belong to them, going to the bars and nightclubs of their choice.

It was a perfect arrangement. Their company in the evenings, I thought, would provide for a lively distraction and needed relief from the varying emotions I was certain to experience during the day.

I was truly touched by my friends' display of friendship and brotherly love.

Even Pam thought it was a great idea.

The following week, José, George, and I met at a Miami travel agency specializing in charter flights to Cuba and booked our airfare for the May 15 flight to Havana. Moments later, however, while still sitting in front of the travel agent, I discovered I had a scheduling conflict that day and moved my date of departure one day forward, to May 16.

After thinking about it for a couple of minutes, my friends decided not to change their flight to match mine—spending an extra night in the forbidden land of fun, rum, and music had proven to be too much of a temptation for them to pass on.

So much for that brotherly love!

George and José had arrived in Havana yesterday and were waiting for me at the Hotel Nacional this morning. I couldn't wait to catch up with them.

"You Don't Know Cuba Very Well Yet, Do You?"

Prior to leaving on my trip, I asked Maidel to find distilled water for me to use during my stay in Cuba. Driving on Havana's busy streets toward the hotel this morning, Maidel informed me that the only place he was able to find something similar to distilled water was in a hospital where one of his many girlfriends worked. He recommended that we stop there on the way to the hotel and pick up a couple of bottles his friend was holding for me.

A few minutes later, we arrived at the hospital and waited for her to join us.

Desperate to use a restroom, I headed toward the nearest building, opened one of its exterior doors, and unknowingly walked into the hospital's oncology wing's patient waiting room. Without air-conditioning or proper ventilation and with the windows rusted and taped shut, the rather large room felt uncomfortably hot. The stench of chemicals, humidity, and sweat filled the air; and traces of mold and mildew clung to its walls and ceiling. Dozens of cancer-stricken patients with IV canisters suspended from portable metallic poles sat uncharacteristically quiet on discolored plastic chairs laid out in neat rows throughout the crowded and strangely quiet room. They sweated profusely and fanned themselves in visible discomfort attempting to simultaneously cool off from the suffocating heat and keep the dozens of flies buzzing around the room from landing on their arms, shoulders, and faces. A small eighteen-inch black-and-white television set with a single rabbit ear antenna was their only distraction.

Through it all, the official government poster of the military-uniformed lady holding her index finger in front of her lips with the text reading "DO NOT RAISE YOUR VOICE" hung on the peeling and stained walls next to the faded and unframed photographs of the Castro brothers and Che Guevara.

The queue line to use the lone toilet room was long. After waiting several minutes and not seeing anyone entering or leaving the single-stall facility, I asked the patient standing in line directly in front of me if anyone had checked to make sure the person using the toilet was well. After all, these were cancer patients, and I feared something could have happened to the person occupying the only toilet room for such a long time.

The patient turned to face me, gave me a long incredulous look, and asked, "You are not from around here, are you?"

"No," I responded.

"Are you from abroad?" he continued.

"Yes," I said, "I'm in line only to use the toilet."

"Don't be concerned," he explained, "there is no one using the toilet right now."

"Then why are we waiting in a line that refuses to move?" I asked naively.

"You don't know Cuba very well yet, do you?" he sighed, "The water here cuts off several times a day. There is no water service at the moment, but it will come back in a few minutes. This is routine. We are all waiting for the water to return."

"In an oncology hospital?" I whispered in disbelief.

"Welcome to Havana, brother," he said softly, trying not to be overheard.

I lost my urge to use the toilet, said goodbye to the unfortunate patient in line with me, and went outside for some fresh air. I had just experienced a glimpse of Cuba's heralded healthcare system and was not impressed. There was no relief for me in the hospital's oncology waiting room's lone toilet this morning—just an initial unimpressive window into Cuba's lamentable reality.

Once outside, I walked toward Maidel and told him what had just happened.

"Mario," he said with a wry smile, "Cuba takes a little getting used to."

"Yes," I responded, "But I think it's probably going to take me a while."

A couple of minutes later, Maidel's girlfriend joined us with two bottles of sterile water. It would be the closest I would get to distilled water in Cuba all week. Getting used to Cuba, I suddenly realized, might take me a little longer than I first thought.

After a brief conversation with his oncologist girlfriend, Maidel and I climbed back into his car, left the hospital's parking lot, and continued our drive toward the Hotel Nacional.

Cruising on the streets of Central Havana for the second time this morning, I stared out the dark-tinted windows of the Chinese sedan and tried to absorb everything Cuban just outside the confines of our car. The images of Havana's old streets, historic architecture, pro-government signs, anti-imperialist billboards, Cuban flags, vintage automobiles, crowded buses, horse-drawn carts, recycled bicycles, and countless pedestrians assured me that I was, in fact, really back in Cuba.

The Hotel Nacional

The magnificent Hotel Nacional de Cuba opened in 1930 with a design style similar to the Breakers and Biltmore American resorts. It is the most storied and prestigious hotel in Cuba and the place where heads of state, American athletes, and movie stars would stay and perform prior to Castro's revolution. The Nacional, with its two lavish cabarets and famous casino, was once partly owned by American gangster Meyer Lansky. Francis Coppola's movie *The Godfather II* was loosely based on real-life gangster events there.

After the 1959 Cuban Revolution, the hotel was primarily used to accommodate visiting diplomats and officials who would sometimes complain that *the walls had ears*. Later on, as a result of the rebirth of foreign tourism to the island, the Hotel Nacional once again started to attract thousands of of travelers from around the world.

This week, it attracted José, George, and me.

Soon after Maidel dropped me off at the Hotel Nacional, my friends caught up with me at the hotel's check-in counter and immediately started peppering me with stories and revelations from their first fun-filled day and night in Cuba. They could not wipe the silly smile from their faces—by now, neither could I.

It was good to see my friends; I felt fortunate to be here with them.

Resolviendo (Hustling) in Cuba

Shortly after checking in, one of the hotel's uniformed cashiers walked up to me and, after looking around to make sure no one was listening, said, "If you need to change your American dollars into Cuban convertible pesos, don't do it at the hotel's bank counter. Come see me in my office and I will give you a better rate of exchange."

I took the cashier up on her offer and, sure enough, received a better exchange rate from her than what was posted at the hotel's bank transaction counter, directly across from her office. I watched in amazement as she withdrew Cuban pesos from her personal purse and replaced them with my dollars. Unbelievably, hotel staff was illicitly functioning as a private bank from inside Cuba's most-storied government-owned hotel.

After taking my suitcase and two warm bottles of sterile water up to my room, it was time for my friends and me to make our way toward the hotel's porte cochere and wait for Maidel to come pick us up in order to start the day's adventures.

Once there, I grew increasingly excited about the imminent start of a journey fifty-six years in the making and reflected on the realization that soon I would be walking on the footprints of my childhood steps in search of the lost pages of my forgotten Cuban story.

I could not wait to get started.

One of the several uniformed doormen hanging around the hotel's porte cochere entrance walked over to meet us, smiled briefly, and said, "Where are you boys from?"

"Florida," my friends and I responded in unison.

"Ah, the Community," he murmured and then added, "Don't take a government-owned taxi. They are old and smell bad. I'll call you a private driver. Their cars are newer, smell better, and will cost you less."

George, José, and I started to laugh. It seemed like all employees at the Hotel Nacional hustled a multitude of services for personal gain with little fear of their government employers.

I had been in Cuba for less than two hours, and the reality of the Cubans' daily struggle to supplement their measly government paycheck was already evident.

Maidel drove his black Chinese sedan with the very dark-tinted windows under the hotel's porte cochere, and my friends and I climbed inside. Minutes later, we were back on the streets of Havana, starting our drive toward the places that once defined my Cuban childhood here.

My Eclectic Family

I stared out the front passenger window of Maidel's car and thought about how my brother and I grew up in Cuba as part of an extended family household that included my parents, maternal grandparents, maternal uncles, and nanny—living, laughing, and breathing as one under the same roof. My brother and I were raised, in one way or another, by all of them in an environment defined by love, music, art, academics, and fun. It was a beautiful time for all of us.

There was never a dull moment in our home, especially after you factor in the eclectic personalities of my family members.

My maternal grandfather, Marcos Mateo, was the patriarch of the family. He was a college-educated and multitalented person whose job as director and auditor of the Casablanca Railroad Station in Havana kept him busy during the week. On weekends, he spent his time painting or crafting an assortment of carpentry projects, including the modernist-style furniture we used in our house. After school, on weekends, and during school breaks, he loved spending time tutoring me in arithmetic and science lessons years ahead of my private school's already challenging curriculum and encouraged me to paint and play with 3D assembly sets daily— unknowingly setting the foundations for my eventual career as an architect. For fun, he played classical guitar and sang. Above all, he was a Mason and adhered to a strict conduct of morality and behavior. I loved him as my second father.

My maternal grandmother, Isaura, was an educator. She stopped teaching school after becoming a mother in order to concentrate on raising and homeschooling my mother and uncles. For fun, my grandmother wrote and published poetry books. An introvert by nature, she was a loving wife and doting grandmother who would often sing along with my grandfather, harmonizing his melodic interpretations. She loved listening to music and sharing her poetry and stories with me. I loved spending time with her.

Their oldest son was my six-foot-one-inch-tall uncle Miguel whose beatnik lifestyle was consistent with the pipe smoking, philosophical thinking, novel reading, and poetry writing antiestablishment Greenwich Village American counterculture movement of the 1950s. He was also an accountant, loved to engage our family in intellectual discussions, and played the flute for fun. His serious demeanor often led to interesting challenges and bantering from his fun-loving brother, Marcolin. I never really understood my uncle Miguel's intellectuality but thought he was mysteriously cool.

My uncle Marcolin was a six-foot-four-inch-tall Jerry Lee Lewis look-alike who loved to play rock and roll and boogie-woogie music on the piano. He was also a doctor. As a result of his intelligence, education, profession, wild ways, musical talent, good looks, and rock and roll piano skills, he was the favorite of every woman he met. His womanizing ways drove my Masonic grandfather, philosophical uncle Miguel, and good-girl mother crazy. Marcolin and I were very close. I understood him and thought he was fun. He always told me he loved me as a son; I loved him as my *other* second father.

My mother, Leida, was my grandparents' middle child. She was the sweet and pretty girl with grace and manners. She loved to play Lecuona compositions and classical music on her piano, write poetry, graduated from college early, and became a kindergarten teacher. She was the yin to Marcolin's yang, the apple of my grandfather's eye, the love of my father's life, and the mother I respected and adored.

My father, Ignacio, was a street-smart kid who lost his father at the tender age of four. Through hard work, tenacity, and iron will, he studied, graduated from college, and became an accountant. After working fifteen years for the Frigidaire Corporation Havana branch office, he established a small accounting practice and mercantile business specializing in the sale of Frigidaire and Sylvania appliances, which he owned until the day we immigrated to the United States. He was athletic, loyal, charismatic, and loved to sing and dance. He could not play an instrument or write poetry but loved baseball and shared his love of the game with me. I grew up with my father as a best friend. We were kindred spirits.

The last member of our clan was my nanny, Marta Lopez. Marta was a patient and sweet Black woman who came to Havana from the countryside looking for work and ended up living with us as another member of our diverse and eclectic clan. I loved her as a second mother. She loved me as her own child.

Living with my extended family meant there was always something to do in my house. Whether it was playing canasta, enjoying my family members playing their instruments, discussing current events, listening to music, or watching baseball games and other programming on television, our times together always included a diverse and exciting menu of activities.

Sometimes, it was great fun just watching my Masonic grandfather keep it together as he discussed the topic-of-the-day with my philosophical uncle Miguel, good-girl mother, and mischievous, sexually liberated uncle Marcolin.

I could not wait to revisit the homes where I grew up living with all of them.

The Place of My Earliest Memories

I had traveled to Cuba seeking to walk on the faded footprints of my childhood in search of the lost memories of my Cuban life. This morning, my journey was about to begin, fittingly, by visiting the place where I took my first steps, located at 454 Carmen Street. This was the house where I lived the first five years of my life, learned about love and family, spoke my initial words, and developed my earliest sense of self. It was the ground where I first stood on my own and the earth where I started to grow my Cuban roots.

Once there, Maidel parked the car alongside the street curb just past the first house I ever called home and turned off the engine, resulting in a most awkward silence. No one said a word inside our car—all eyes were on me.

Nervously trying to absorb the sights around us, I glanced at the side passenger mirror and noticed the simultaneous reflections of my childhood home and adult face. The place where I lived the earliest years of my life stared back at me seemingly unchanged; only my reflection in the mirror showed the passage of time.

My middle-aged face, however, did not belong with the reflection of my house at Carmen Street; the likeness of my earliest childhood years growing up in this house did. Buoyed by this most beautiful realization, I stepped out of the car and walked onto my former home's still-manicured yard, stopping just short of the front door.

Standing on the front walk of my former home on Carmen Street—overwhelmed by countless powerful nostalgic emotions—I looked around and tried to absorb the increasingly familiar images now surrounding me. Beautiful and heartfelt memories of my time in this house suddenly started to return, including the long-forgotten sensations of love and wonder synonymous with the innocence of my years living here.

I remembered standing on this same sidewalk dressed in my off-white-and-brown school uniform with the *Instituto Edison's* logo on my chest, waiting for my father to drive me to school. I recalled playing cowboys and Indians with my brother and neighborhood friends here, reenacting scenes from those American movies and television shows I often watched. I thought about how I would often play fetch and tousle with our pet terrier, Terry, on the front lawn of this house, much to my grandmother's delight. I remembered learning how to throw and catch a baseball with my father in front of this house as well, earning his loving and proud praise for my efforts.

Life was good here once.

I had not traveled to Havana empty-handed today. Rummaging through a few of my family's photo albums in my Fort Lauderdale home before embarking on this trip, I found several black-and-white photographs taken during my childhood in this house, illustrating not just the joy and innocence of my youngest years but also what my former home on Carmen Street looked like during the early 1950s. I placed them, along with other vintage photos from my life in Cuba, in a three-ring notebook and brought them with me.

Comparing those old photographs to the house in front of me today proved that not much had changed here since then. The doors, windows, balconies, and railings still looked like those in the photos I brought. The granite trim on the front walk to the house, visible in the photograph of me posing on my first day of kindergarten, was similarly unchanged. Astonishingly, even the ancient metal plate house number on the front porch wall was the original as seen in my baby photograph taken here in 1951.

(Circa 1955) In front of my home on Carmen Street dressed in my school's uniform and ready for my first day of kindergarten

They say you can never go home again. In Cuba, however, a place stuck in 1959 and encased in a continuum, you come close. A rush of awareness confirmed that my time here was real. I once lived in this house. I was, in fact, Cuban.

George snapped several pictures while I posed in positions matching the old photographs I had brought with me. The neighbors—now outside their homes—smiled, shook their heads, and stared at us as if we were a comedy act. I felt like a kid again, and probably acted as one, as I imitated those innocent poses from long ago.

Earlier this morning, I was boarding my chartered flight in Miami; barely three hours later, George and I were laughing hysterically in front of my first home in Havana—surprisingly unchanged. I had flown into a place frozen in a time warp, incredibly preserving the initial footsteps of my life.

I had traveled to Cuba in search of my earliest childhood memories; instead, they had started finding me.

The elderly woman living in my former home walked out of her house onto the front porch to see what my friends and I were doing in her front yard. I walked toward her, said hello, and introduced myself. I told her I had come here seeking to retrace the earliest years of my life living in this house in hopes of regaining the forgotten memories, colors, and humanity of my lost Cuban years. She looked at me curiously, shrugged her shoulders, and did not respond.

Undaunted, I showed her really cute photographs of me as a baby and young child living in this house and explained how excited I was that today, for the first time in decades, I had started to recall memories I once thought did not exist. She glanced at my childhood photographs with a cold and distant expression, rolled her eyes in dramatic fashion, and fixed her stare over my shoulders toward the neighbors—still outside their homes behind me.

Having nothing to lose and much to gain, I asked her the question she probably sensed was coming anyway, "Would you be kind enough to tour me through your home? It might help me regain some additional memories. Would you please help me recall?"

She raised her left eyebrow, gave me a long disinterested look, and simply said, "No!"

I slowed my heartbeat and told myself I was fine. To her, I was probably just an irritating stranger from the United States. I could see how my request to enter her house might have been interpreted as intrusive or perhaps even nefarious. I convinced myself to try again some other day.

My return to the front yard of the unchanged home of my earliest years, however, had already served as a most rewarding start to what I hoped would be a week of fulfilling discoveries, returning memories, and gaining closures denied.

Tricycle Days

José, George, and I climbed inside Maidel's black Chinese sedan with the dark-tinted windows and started the very short drive to Mendosa Park, our second stop today.

My nanny, Marta, would bring me to this park daily when I was a toddler, eventually changing our visits to the weekends once I started school. I had many wonderful memories of playing with the neighborhood kids and spending time with Marta in this park—a child's wonderland I always claimed to have bought for a penny.

I could hardly wait to see it again.

Once my friends and I arrived at Mendosa Park, I recognized it immediately. I walked up its wide entry steps and past the grassy play area until reaching the winding walks that eventually ended at the concrete oval rink where I always rode my tricycle—my favorite place in the park. Amazingly, just like the house on Carmen Street, not much seemed to have changed here since the last time I saw it as a small child either. Even the trees around me looked old enough to date back to the days I once played here as a toddler.

The sun always seemed to shine during our visits to Mendosa Park. It felt good to enjoy my childhood sun once more.

I missed my tricycle today.

(Circa 1954) Riding my tricycle at Mendosa Park

I thought about how Marta, not having children of her own, lovingly called me *"mi niñito"* (my little boy). Our days spent in

Mendosa Park were always special times for us. She would cheer for me while I rode my tricycle on the oval rink or played with the neighborhood kids—often joining in on the fun.

I had a photograph in my three-ring binder of her holding me atop a decorative pedestal fountain here. I tried to find the fountain today, only to learn from a local resident that it was severely damaged during a hurricane some time ago and subsequently needed to be demolished. It saddened me.

I recalled how Marta and I would often have lunch together in this park. Getting me to stop playing in order to sit and eat lunch was sometimes a challenging task. Today, I remembered for the first time in decades her little secret for getting me to eat my meals here.

"I will buy you chocolate ice cream after lunch, *mi niñito*," she would tell me, "if you promise to eat all your lunch."

Her bribes worked well. How could I refuse? I never disappointed her.

Marta unfortunately passed away several years ago. Visiting this park reminded me of her beautiful face, sweet demeanor, and the pure love we had for each other. It was good to remember her gentle and loving warm embrace—a tenderness I had not felt for far too long.

I missed Marta today.

My friends and I bought chocolate ice cream cones from the ancient ice cream shop Marta and I frequently visited after I successfully finished my meals here—still across from Mendosa Park after all these years—and carefully slid into Maidel's car, trying as best we could not to make a mess.

Once safely inside, Maidel started driving us to my Sevillano home, our next planned stop this morning.

(Circa 1952) Sitting on Mendosa Park's decorative
pedestal fountain next to my loving nanny Marta.

A Dubious Stranger

The search for my Sevillano home's address at 90½ Cervantes
Street, in a district of Havana with no street signs, proved to be
an interesting and educational journey into the world of modern
Cuban-style paranoia.

One of the ways the Cuban system polices its citizens today,
is by encouraging and rewarding neighborhood accusations. A
complaint against a neighbor can often result in a reward for the

accuser and punishment for the accused. As a result, Cubans are careful of what they say in public and often wary of strangers.

Driving through the rugged Sevillano District roads in our shiny new Chinese sedan today, qualified us as the most dubious of strangers. Attempting to find the three-block-long Cervantes Street, Maidel continually approached anyone we could and asked for directions, only to be repeatedly ignored. One look at the four of us inside our most ominous official-looking black sedan with the very dark-tinted windows generated responses consisting of a shrug of the shoulders, a tilt of the head, or a simple "I don't know." Others sheepishly claimed not to be locals even though they were carrying perishable groceries with them.

Unable to find Cervantes Street, Maidel informed us that he would attempt to borrow a GPS device from a friend overnight and try again tomorrow. We all agreed and decided to leave the Sevillano District and drive toward the last home I lived in Cuba, located at 359 San Leonardo Street.

The Year of Broken Dreams

During the early 1950s, my family rented our homes in the Carmen and Sevillano Districts of Havana. By early 1959, with my father's business growing increasingly prosperous and our family finances improving accordingly, we bought a new house being built in a single-family suburban development called Reparto Apolo.

Our time living there, however, did not last long. Soon after my father signed the contract to buy the Apolo house, the winds of political change swept over the island, suffocating it with waves of broken dreams and changes incompatible with our future lives in Cuba. By November 1960, my parents, brother, and I would emigrate from our Apolo home to the United States.

My grandparents, however, continued to live there, hopeful for the day of our return—a family reunification never destined to be.

My friends and I had no problem finding San Leonardo Street and my Apolo house this afternoon—I recognized it as soon as we drove past it. Maidel parked our car about a block away, and the four of us started walking toward my former home.

Halfway there, the memories of my life here started to return all at once, filling me with overpowering feelings of joy and youthful anticipation that took me by surprise. I stopped walking, took a deep breath, calmed myself down, and gave in to my irresistible nostalgic instincts.

I thought about how my years living in this house were defined by preteen impulses that often led me into daring and reckless adventures and misadventures—I chose never to tell my children for fear of setting a bad example.

Living here, I learned to stretch my wings as far as they would go. I remember those days as a time of great discovery, exploration, wonder, and fun; my parents, I am sure, would still refer to them as "Mario's challenging years."

Memories of My Preteen Adventures and Misadventures from My Apolo Years

Let's chase the fumigation truck! I remembered how I would often chase the menacing black mosquito-control fumigation trucks whenever they drove past our Apolo home, screaming at them until they drove out of sight. Those imposing and ominous bug-killing machines would slowly chug up the hill road in front of our house with a racket and attitude difficult for a young boy to ignore. To me, they always seemed like dragons invading our street, cowardly fading into the same fog of pesticide they spewed.

I couldn't help but smile at the memory of my grandmother's perplexed looks whenever she scolded me for chasing those poisonous trucks—and laugh at the innocent mindlessness of my preteen dragon-slaying heroics.

Who wants to jump on a slow-moving train? My Apolo home sits on top of a hill. Its backyard slopes down onto a cattle ranch, creek, and finally, railroad tracks beyond. I thought about how one day my older cousin Julio and I ran down the hill, climbed a mango tree next to the ranch's perimeter fence, and decided to practice our baseball pitching by throwing mangoes at the steers grazing on the rancher's property below us. After a while, the bulls grew unhappy with the mangoes being thrown their way and moved to the other end of the farm. Not knowing what to do next, we sat on one of the tree's upper branches and looked around for something else to do. The sight and sounds of an old cargo steam train hissing, smoking, clanging, and chugging its way down the railroad tracks toward us got our attention. Sensing an opportunity too irresistible to miss, Julio and I climbed down the mango tree, ran toward the tracks, and for reasons obvious only to an eight-year-old decided to jump on one of the slow-moving train's flatbed cars. This, we thought, would be the beginning of a great adventure.

Soon, however, the train gained speed, and neither of us dared to jump off. About an hour later and miles away from home, the train finally reached its next stop. My cousin and I strategically moved behind the cargo sharing the flatbed with us, jumped off the train onto the tracks below, and walked ever so slowly toward the train station— trying hard not to be noticed. Not having any money, we knew we would have to ask someone for a coin to insert into one of the station's payphones in order to call one of our parents for help. A sweet-looking grandmother proved the perfect target. Since neither Julio nor I wanted to sacrifice our future freedom by being the one calling home, we decided to use our new coin to flip for the "honor." Unfortunately, I lost. I had no choice, then, but to call my father and ask him to come pick us up. My dad, needless to say, was not amused. Once we got home, our greatest adventure ended with dual parental lectures and separate father-mandated in-bedroom incarcerations for Julio and me.

The adventure, I remember thinking at the time, was still worth it; I am certain our parents would still disagree.

Why are you bringing an axe? I also remembered how, another time, Julio and I climbed a nearby hill pretending to be US marines exploring a hilltop forest. For some unknown reason, Julio brought an axe with him that morning and decided to use it on a fallen tree branch resting on the trail we were walking on. Over and over, he chopped down on that log until one of his mighty swings missed the target, landing instead on his little toe—resulting in much blood and loud screams. I placed his arm around my shoulders and, like a courageous World War II hero, bravely helped him down the hill and across imaginary enemy lines toward the safety of his family's home.

Everything went as planned, except for his bloody toe. For my "bravery" that afternoon, however, I was rewarded with another parental safety lecture and in-bedroom incarceration.

"Mario Cartaya Mateo, I Have Been Waiting for You a Long Time"

But those memories were then, and this was now. I focused on the sight of my former Apolo home, grew excited at my impending return to the last house I once called home in Cuba, and started my final approach toward it.

I remembered once learning that a man named Hector had moved into my former house after my grandfather passed away in 1967. I looked forward to meeting him and hoped he could provide me with stories about my family's life during the years following our departure from Cuba, his relationship with my grandparents and uncles, and how he came to live in our Apolo house.

I hoped he was home this morning.

A few steps later, I noticed a man standing behind my former home's chain-link gate, lost in conversation with two other persons on the sidewalk in front of him. Once my friends and I caught up with them, the two men on the sidewalk acknowledged us with a nod of their heads, excused themselves, and walked away.

The man inside the gate, however, turned his body to face us and smiled. I smiled back, shook his hand, and said, "Good morning."

"Good morning to you too," he replied.

I paused for a moment, cleared my throat, and softly asked, "Is your name Hector?"

"Yes," he answered politely, "and you are?"

"Mario Cartaya Mateo," I responded, using my paternal and maternal surnames for family identification.

Hector gave me a long look, smiled broadly, walked through the gate onto the sidewalk next to me, and said, "Mario Cartaya Mateo, I have been waiting for you a long time."

I had prepared myself to expect the unexpected during this trip and knew I would face moments that would challenge me, but Hector's greeting was different than anything I could have ever imagined.

I just stood there, on the sidewalk in front of my Apolo house, and looked at him completely dumbfounded; I had no idea what he meant.

"Mario, what was that about?" José whispered in my ear.

"I don't know," I responded.

"This is going to be fun," George summed up for all of us.

I opened my three-ring notebook and showed Hector several black-and-white photographs, taken in 1960, of my grandparents, parents, and uncles standing on the front porch of my former home. He stared at them with much delight, started to laugh, and said, "Mayito, I knew your family well. Your grandfather, Marcos, was a good man. I loved him very much."

"I loved him too," I said.

"Your uncle Marcolin," he said, "was so tall that the top of my head barely reached his shoulders. He was my best friend, you know."

"We were very close," he continued, "like brothers."

Astonishingly, I was face-to-face with a man who had known, interacted with, and loved my family. Hector was the first tangible human connection with the family members I once left behind in this house fifty-six years ago, never to see again. There was much I needed to ask him.

Realizing the importance of this serendipitous moment, I took a deep breath, shelved my emotions, and nervously asked, "Hector, what did you mean when you greeted me with, 'I have been waiting for you a long time?'"

"You don't know, do you?" he asked incredulously. "When your uncle Marcolin discovered that your grandfather's illness was terminal, he did not want your house to be confiscated by the government and assigned to a military officer or political crony upon his death, so he allowed my wife and me to move into your family's home. I, in turn, agreed to take care of your house and family's possessions until the day you returned from the United States, at which time I would give it all back to you."

"No one would have thought it would have taken so long for us to meet," I interjected, "but I am only visiting today. I did not come to stay."

"It's good you are here. Please come inside your house with me. There are some things I want to show you," Hector concluded and led my friends and me into my former home.

The Lonely Silence of Tangible Evidence

Once inside the living room, Hector placed one of his arms around my shoulders, smiled proudly, and said, "Look around. Do you recognize anything?"

"Yes, I do," I responded, recalling every door, room, and window around me. The Cuban time warp was alive and well in my Apolo home too. Even the floor tiles and wall colors were the original finishes from when I lived here in 1960—nothing had changed.

"Look again," he continued. "Is there anything else here you remember?"

"Everything looks so familiar," I murmured, nervously attempting to absorb the many images from my past now surrounding me.

"Look at the furniture," he mentioned. "Your grandfather built it."

"Yes, I remember now," I wistfully responded, as memories of my grandfather working on his many carpentry projects returned all at once. "He built them just before we moved into this house."

"Now look inside the curio adjacent to the dining room table," he instructed me.

I walked over to the curio my grandfather built years ago and bent over to have a better look inside its glass top and sliding glass doors.

"These were our utensils and dishes!" I exclaimed with surprising delight.

"Yes, they are," he said. "No one has touched them since the day your grandfather died."

Hector had amazingly kept a promise he made my uncle Marcolin five decades ago. Our home, as well as the contents stored inside, was still here quietly awaiting my family's return from our life in exile in the United States.

In front of me once again, astonishingly untouched during the last fifty years, were the furniture and household goods synonymous with my life in this house. The living room and dining room furniture designed and built by my grandfather—as well as the drinking glasses, coffee cups, pastel-colored 1950s

Jell-O bowls, dishes, and dining utensils my family and I used daily—stared at me in lonely silence.

Tangible evidence of everyday items from my preteen years was suddenly within my reach once more. An immense wave of nostalgia swept over me.

I slowly opened the sliding glass doors on the face of my grandfather's modernist curio, gently reached inside, and once again touched my past.

I recognized my uncle Marcolin's favorite beer glass and pulled it off its glass shelf. I remembered how, every Sunday prior to our weekly family dinner, my father and uncles sat on the front porch of our Apolo house to share stories, tell jokes, and snack on saltine crackers with sardines while ceremoniously washing them down with cold beer. Marcolin was the only one who drank his beer out of a glass—the same art deco, polka-dotted glass I was now holding ever so tightly in my hand.

I asked Hector for permission to keep my uncle's old beer glass and gave it to Maidel to safely store inside his car. I eventually took the glass—and the Apolo memories of my uncle Marcolin— back with me to the United States.

"I really like your uncle Marcolin's beer glass," George joked.

"Well, maybe I'll let you drink out of it someday," I said, "but you have to bring the beer."

Echoes of My Family's Banter, Baseball Broadcasts, and More

Hector asked my friends and me to join him and his family in the living room. We sat on the sofa and chairs designed and built by my grandfather when I was a little boy and listened with great joy to Hector's recollections about his life in Cuba and the friendship he once shared with my family.

Visibly emotional, you could hear the excitement and joy in his voice with every story he told. His lively recollections resonated from the walls of my former Apolo house—serving as a fitting foreground to the memory and echoes of my family's banter, music, and laughter that long ago transformed this house into my home.

Today, the memories, sights, and sounds of my childhood here were alive within me as my friends and I shared an improbable afternoon with a newly discovered family friend—an incredibly loyal and decent man named Hector.

Eventually, Hector asked me to go on a tour of the house with him while my friends remained in the living room sharing stories and a pitcher of cold lemonade with his family.

We walked toward my former bedroom and opened its door. The sight of my room's wood jalousie windows flanked by the built-in display cases that once held my school's academic awards and Legion of Honor sash made me smile. Below these windows, I would often lie in bed secretly listening to the play-by-play radio broadcasts of Almendares or Cuban Sugar King baseball games at night, keeping the volume low enough so as not to allow my parents to find out what I was doing when I should have been sleeping.

They probably knew anyway. I would often fall asleep during the baseball broadcasts only to wake up to a radio that had magically turned itself off in the middle of the night.

After leaving my old bedroom, Hector and I continued walking through the rest of the house, eventually stopping in front of a locked door. He reached into one of his pockets, brought out a set of keys, and opened it. "Do you remember this room?" he asked.

"Yes," I responded, "this was my grandparents' bedroom."

"You are right," he said. "Please walk into this room with me. There is something I want to show you."

"Your grandfather died on this bed," Hector informed me while pointing to the queen-size bed in the middle of the room.

I had always believed my grandfather passed away in a hospital. To find out he died at home, on a bed I could now touch, was something I never expected.

I walked into my grandparents' former bedroom and stared at the bed where my grandfather died. Fighting back the tears that wanted to appear, I looked away from Hector, not wanting him to notice my discomfort.

"No one has slept on that bed since your grandfather's death," Hector sighed. "He suffered greatly during his illness, you know. Once it became evident that the end was near and his pain had grown too intense to bear, I watched as your uncle Marcolin administered several doses of morphine to your grandfather inside this room in a desperate effort to control his pain."

Hector was right. My uncle had confided the same to me years ago and asked me never to tell anyone, least of all my mother.

I sat on my grandfather's bed, gently touched his pillow with my hand, and contemplated the horrific scene that must have once transpired here. I sensed my grandfather's plight in this room— realizing death was coming and he would never see us again. An indescribable sorrow filled my heart.

I thought about how difficult it was for my mother to accept her father's death without being able to see him, comfort him, or tell him how much she loved him. I remembered how, distraught and brokenhearted, she cried for weeks in our Miami home. I am sure my grandparents, uncles, and aunts cried for weeks in this Havana bedroom as well.

Today, it was my turn to say goodbye to my grandfather while sitting on his deathbed—consoled by the memory of my family's love and a new friend named Hector.

I missed my grandfather today.

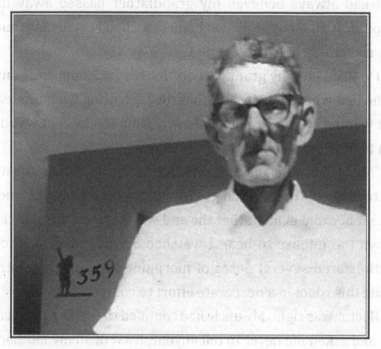

(Circa 1960) My grandfather, Marcos Mateo, on our Apolo home's porch in front of the house number I once selected.

A Secret Well Kept

Just before we immigrated to the United States, my father agreed to sell his business to his junior partner for a total of thirteen thousand pesos (still on a par with the American dollar in 1960). By then, however, the Cuban government was already limiting the flow of currency toward the United States to no more than one hundred dollars per family. As a result, the proceeds from the sale of my father's business would have to remain in Havana.

Soon after the sale agreement was executed—requiring the buyer to deliver the proceeds in cash to my grandfather at our Apolo home—my parents, brother, and I fled Cuba to the United States. The plan was for my grandfather to care for the money until our return from what we all thought would be a short-lived exile.

As the years unfolded and our exile became permanent, we never received confirmation in Miami that my grandfather ever received the cash in Havana. After his death, the issue fell forever silent. My father always believed his ex-partner never made the payment, keeping the money for himself.

Hector helped me walk away from my grandfather's bedroom and asked me to follow him outside the house toward the side yard. He had one more place to show me today.

Once there, he looked at me and softly, so as not to be overheard by his neighbors, asked, "Do you recognize this concrete walk?"

"No, I don't," I responded.

"No, you wouldn't remember it," he said. "I poured it at your uncle's request after you left for the United States."

"Why are you showing me this sidewalk?" I asked.

"Do you see that mark?" he said, pointing at a visible scar on the concrete walk. "Beneath it, your uncle Marcolin buried thirteen thousand old Cuban pesos in wax-filled cans just after you and your family left for the United States. He told me it was Cuban currency from your father's business sale."

"How come no one ever informed us in Miami that the payment from the sale of my father's business was made?" I asked.

"Your grandfather never sent you confirmation he received the money because he feared government retaliation. Soon after your departure, all dollar-based Cuban pesos had to be returned to the government for replacement with the new currency, worthless in value outside Cuba. Failure to do so was illegal. Anyone found in possession of the old currency could end up in jail."

"So he never told anyone?" I asked.

"No one," Hector replied. "This money is yours. I will dig it out and give it to you right now if you want it."

"No," I said. "Let it stay buried here as a lasting memory of my grandfather and a tribute to an honest and loyal friend who kept his promise to care for our house and the money he was entrusted to care for until the day of our return."

My father had been wrong all these years. He died in Miami still believing his ex-partner betrayed him. I wish he would have known the truth. It would have saved him considerable heartbreak, bitterness, and pain.

Hector and I walked back into the house and joined my friends, now standing and mingling with his family in the living room, just in time to enjoy the last glasses of cold lemonade being served by his wife.

Loyalty, Honor, and Gratitude

I thought about how Hector had lived with his family in this house for five decades, honoring the promise he made my uncle Marcolin to protect and maintain our home and personal property until the day of our return, never giving in to the temptation to sell any of it in order to help his family during Cuba's many periods of severe shortages.

Who keeps that kind of promise for fifty years? Hector, an honest and loyal family friend, did. I, on the other hand, spent all that time enjoying the benefits and opportunities of a middle-class life in the United States. I realized I had no moral right to claim this house any longer. I knew what I had to do.

I walked up to Hector, shook his hand, and said, "You are an honorable and loyal friend who kept a promise to my family during most of your adult life. I am honored to have met you. Your promise to the Mateo family is now fulfilled. I want this to be your home now."

"Thank you," he responded, his voice cracking with great emotion.

"Mario," George said as he placed his arm across my shoulders, "you are a good man."

Hector hugged me, kissed me on the cheek, and softly whispered, "Only until the day of my death. After I die, I want you to have your home back, no questions asked. Your grandfather and uncle Marcolin would have wanted it that way."

Leaving My Apolo House — Again

By now it was already the middle of the afternoon, and my friends and I needed to move on to our next stop.

The last time I left my Apolo home, I was fleeing my country of birth and leaving my loved ones behind. There was considerable pain and anguish that day as we closed the front door behind us.

There was no suffering leaving the Apolo house today, just the realization that our home had been well taken care of by a good man who, against all odds, had kept our family's possessions, memories, and legacy alive for fifty years.

I hugged Hector once more and told him it was time for my friends and me to go. I promised to visit him again someday soon; after all, he was family now. My friends and I stepped out my former home's front door, waved goodbye to a teary-eyed Hector, and walked toward Maidel's car.

It was time to go.

Visiting my Apolo home today was a sobering reminder of my family's difficult departure from Cuba, the anticipation of a prompt return, my grandfather's last days here, and the integrity of the man my uncle chose to care for our home during our exile. It was a sad testament to the abusive, corrupt, and chaotic early days of Castro's revolution and the horrific systematic family separations that continues to define the Cuban Diaspora today.

It was also a tale of Cuban brotherhood, family ties, loyalty, and honesty spanning the Florida Straits and conquering the test of time—a beautiful story of hope for a future inclusive of Cuban reconciliation.

"Never underestimate the power of
dreams and the influence of the human spirit."
Wilma Rudolph

(May, 2016) With Hector and his wife in front of the
Apolo house curio built built by my grandfather

Back to School

Minutes later, my friends and I were back on the streets of
Havana again, making our way toward the *Instituto Edison*—the
private school I attended from prekindergarten through the fourth
grade and played such an important part of my Cuban childhood.

For years, I struggled with fragmented memories of my time
there, often waking up from dreams about my Edison school days
in impotent frustration. Today, I sought to retrace the childhood
steps I once took in my former school in hopes of regaining those

memories that might help me complete my partial dreams. I couldn't wait to get there.

I remembered how my father once asked my brother and me not to let anyone in school know we were leaving Cuba for the United States in order to avoid the ridicule, insults, and acts of violence common during those days against Cubans fleeing the country. One November afternoon in 1960, I silently walked out of my school's fourth-grade classroom and never looked back.

Today, I was returning to my school for the first time since that day.

By the time we arrived at the *Instituto Edison* this afternoon, the school day was starting to wind down. I stepped out of Maidel's car, took a deep breath, and started walking with George toward the school's beautiful marbled school entry portico I remembered with so much love.

Once we got there, I was happy to discover that the original 1930s "*Instituto Edison*" inscription carved into the portico's facade, as well as the "I.E." granite floor logo below it, were unchanged. I had not expected to see either of them today; the American names and logos of many schools, public venues and streets in Havana were unceremoniously replaced with names, titles, and symbols synonymous with the Cuban Revolution long ago. It was good to realize my school was not one of them.

Close to a dozen school-uniformed boys, about the same age I was when I left Cuba, were talking and laughing underneath the school's portico as George and I approached it this afternoon. Once the boys saw us coming, they awkwardly settled down, made eye contact with us, and flashed their best I-didn't-do-anything-wrong smiles. For a magical and beautiful moment, it felt like my former school friends were here once more—patiently waiting for me to start our school day together.

It was a fitting way to start my return visit to the school I always felt so connected with.

We found the school's administration wing, walked inside, and asked the receptionist if we could speak with the school principal.

The receptionist looked at us, winked, and said, "Do you mean the head administrator?"

"Yes," I responded. "Could we please speak with her?"

"Of course, follow me," she answered and led us into her office.

Once there, the tall Afro-Cuban head administrator stood up from behind her desk and politely asked, "Brothers, how can I help you today?"

"I attended the *Instituto Edison* during the 1950s, and my mother taught kindergarten here in the 1940s and 1950s," I said. "As a matter of fact, the mural painting in the kindergarten room was painted by my grandfather long ago. Would you allow me to walk around the school in order to remember my years here?"

"I did not attend school here," George added with a wink and a smile, "but my mother did. Can I go with Mario too?"

"Brothers, there are still some students finishing their school day or attending after-school programs," the head administrator said. "The only way I can let you in is with an escort. Would that be okay?"

"Sure," I responded.

She called the school's security guard and asked him to give us a tour of the school. Moments later, a young man named Bruno walked over to us, introduced himself as our guide, and started to lead us out of the administration wing's offices.

Just a few steps into our tour, however, the head administrator unexpectedly caught up with us, flashed a sad smile, and said, "*Compañero* [comrade], I am sorry to tell you that your grandfather's mural was painted over two years ago when we refinished the school classrooms' walls."

"Comrade?" I suddenly remembered where I was.

I said goodbye to the head administrator, left the administration wing mourning the loss of my grandfather's mural and proceeded to walk with George and Bruno toward the school's main classroom building.

Halfway there, our young guide received a call on his cell phone, turned to look at George and me, and apologetically muttered, "Please forgive me, but my girlfriend just called and I need to leave. You two go on with your walk. Just don't do anything stupid. Don't get me into any trouble. Have fun, brothers."

George and I said goodbye to Bruno and watched him walk away still talking on his cell phone.

Free to explore the *Instituto Edison* on our own, we suddenly found ourselves mindlessly walking through the eerily familiar corridors of my former school, briefly entering the kindergarten classroom I attended with my mother as my teacher—and the student cafeteria where I often enjoyed *media noche* sandwiches, *mariquita* chips, and *Ironbeer* soft drinks for lunch. We climbed the stairway leading to the second-floor corridor and started to walk past dozens of students hurriedly entering and leaving their classrooms. Most of them briefly stared at us and smiled; others simply said hello.

Impulsively, I opened a random second floor classroom door and entered it. Luckily, no one was inside. I looked around and immediately realized just how well I knew this room—it took my breath away.

"Welcome to the Fourth Grade," read the ancient, faded sign above the old-fashioned chalkboard behind the teacher's desk. Somehow, against all odds, I had unexpectedly wandered back inside the same fourth-grade classroom I silently left one November day in 1960, never to return ... until today!

Trying to make sense of this most incredible coincidence, I sat on one of the classroom's vintage wooden desks with the metal hinged top above the frontal book storage bin I remembered so well from my days as a student here and stared at my former fourth-grade classroom in utter amazement and disbelief.

I knew this place. Everything looked—and smelled—like the fourth-grade classroom I once left ever so silently toward a new life in the United States. For a delicious moment, I felt like I was nine years old again, wearing my school's off-white-and-brown uniform with the I.E. logo over my heart, quietly seated on my assigned desk waiting for my teacher and classmates to walk in at any minute. I was back in school.

Astonishingly, my former classroom had welcomed me back today, not just as a curious adult rediscovering his past but rather as a child returning to his classroom after what now seemed more like a long vacation than fifty-six years spent in exile. It was a most beautiful and tender experience.

A few minutes later, it was time to leave my fourth-grade classroom once more. Looking for a place to exhale and come to grips with my most unexpected emotions, I decided to walk with George toward my school's ceremonial exterior courtyard in search of a little fresh air.

The *Instituto Edison's* courtyard once was a multipurpose exterior plaza where school functions, recognitions, and festivals were celebrated throughout the year. It was also the place where students and teachers held a daily morning preschool ritual that included singing the school's alma mater hymn and Cuban national anthem while the student honor guard ceremoniously hoisted the Cuban and *Instituto Edison* flags.

Other than the baseball field, this courtyard was my favorite part of the school. It was, after all, a place of great fun, rewards, and exploration. I stood next to George in the middle of the courtyard, thought about the many times I lined up with my classmates here to start a new school day, and instinctively started to softly sing the Cuban national anthem and school's hymn. Surprisingly, even though I had not sung them for decades, I remembered the words.

George looked at me in quiet bewilderment, briefly shook his head, and said, "Dude, what are you doing?"

"Starting our school day," I answered.

"Okay," he said, "let's go terrorize the teachers."

"Sounds like fun," I concluded. "Let's go!"

My unanticipated school morning ritual now completed; I opened my three-ring notebook and started to compare the buildings surrounding the courtyard today with the 1950s photographs I had brought from home. It was good to see that except for some minor repairs, lack of paint, and missing landscaping, everything still looked remarkably similar to their images on my vintage pictures.

I stared at an especially poignant photograph of my brother and me dressed in our cowboy and Superman costumes standing in this courtyard during a school festival in 1957. My brother passed away several years ago, but his memory stood next to me in the middle of our school's courtyard once again today.

So much has changed in my life, I thought. *So little had changed in this school.*

George and I left the school's ceremonial courtyard and headed toward the Baccalaureate Center, a building of significant architectural praise, where my brother last attended high school classes here. Once there, we methodically explored as many of the upper level classrooms as we could sneak into, attempting to retrace the shadows of my brother's footsteps from long ago—trying hard not to get caught.

My brother never got to say goodbye to his high school classrooms. This afternoon, George and I did it for him.

I missed my brother today.

(Circa 1956) With my older brother in our school's courtyard

The Games Never Played

Not to brag, but I was a pretty good baseball player. Being only eight years old, however, unfortunately meant I was too young to play in league games with my school's team even though I was allowed to practice with the older players on the field. I dreamed of the day I would wear my school's off-white baseball uniform with the cursive "Edison" emblazoned in brown across my chest. Those dreams ended the day I immigrated to the United States.

George and I left the Baccalaureate Center, walked over to the school's baseball field, and sat on the concrete bleachers parallel the third base foul line. I thought about the many times I practiced on the clay infield below, moving with the crack of the bat to catch the balls hit my way during infield drills and hitting baseballs during batting practice. Looking at the ballfield today, I suddenly realized that even though I never got to wear the *Instituto Edison* baseball uniform representing my school, I had never felt any regrets.

My baseball memories here, it turned out, were always enough to sustain me.

Weeks before traveling to Cuba, I discovered that one of my college friends attended the *Instituto Edison* during the same years I was there. Being a little older than me, he was already playing on the school's baseball team. Had I stayed in Cuba long enough to reach the minimum age requirements, we would have surely become *Instituto Edison* baseball teammates—a destiny denied once we both fled the island.

We did, however, become friends and teammates on an unforgettable softball team at the University of Florida that would win over one hundred consecutive games, undefeated in a span of over three years. Heck, we even challenged and beat the University of Florida's baseball team.

I wished my college friend and I could have played catch on the *Instituto Edison's* baseball field today.

Rediscovering My School Days

My returning memories at the *Instituto Edison* today included not just what occurred at a specific place on campus during my time as a student here but also how I perceived it through the innocence of my childhood. All afternoon, the context of my memories vacillated among the discipline of my school days, limited perspective and understanding as a child, desire to please authority, and the expectations of my family. It was beautiful and rewarding to feel the dreams and hopes from my years of childhood wonder as a student here once more.

It was a great gift.

No Need for a Silent Departure Today

Unlike in 1960, I did not want to leave the *Instituto Edison* silently today. On our way out, George and I stopped at the administration office wing and met with the head administrator once more.

"Thank you for allowing us to visit my school," I said. "It was extremely beautiful and rewarding."

"I'm glad I could help you, brother," she answered.

"Last time I was here, it was safest for me to leave without letting anyone know," I said. "Today, I want to say a goodbye fifty-six years overdue."

"It's never too late, *compañero*. You are welcome here anytime," she said.

I gave her a hug and said goodbye; she hugged me back and smiled.

George and I joined José and Maidel in front of the school, climbed back into the black Chinese sedan with the dark-tinted windows, and left the *Instituto Edison* toward my father's former business address on *La Calzada 10 de Octubre* boulevard—once the center of commerce and former prestigious address for restaurants, hotels, theaters, and businesses in Havana.

Researching family documents and photographs prior to leaving on this trip, I stumbled upon a telegram addressed to my father, dated September 1960, while he was in the United States trying to secure employment prior to our planned November departure from Cuba. The telegram confirmed the sale of his business identified by an address that matched my mother's recollection of its former location. Armed with this information, Maidel found my father's former office and walked inside with me.

A Future Safety No Longer Guaranteed

My father had waited a long time to start his private business specializing in accounting services and appliance sales for American-made Frigidaire and Sylvania products. He had high hopes for its financial future and, as a result, a better life for our family. Those dreams were crushed in 1960, however, as the political situation in Cuba grew increasingly unstable and the government sought to nationalize American properties throughout the island.

Standing inside my father's former business this afternoon, I imagined the day that two machine gun-toting rebels unexpectedly barged through its front doors aggressively demanding his company's accounting ledgers containing the locations of his American clients' properties, facilities, and products throughout Cuba. I thought about how his brave refusal to cooperate with his transgressors that day led to his detention and subsequent interrogation until finally, with his life in real and imminent danger, he grudgingly agreed to hand over the records they sought.

By then, however, he was unfortunately blacklisted and warned by the lead interrogator that his future safety in Cuba was no longer guaranteed, ushering in the beginning of the end of our lives here.

It saddened me to think how my father was denied his dreams and once-promising future as a result of geopolitical events he had no interest in or control over. I wished things would have turned out differently.

After Sunset

As the sun started to set on what had been a long and exciting first day in Cuba, my friends and I headed back to the hotel to shower, dress, go out to dinner, and make our presence felt at one of the local nightclubs.

Today had been a day of great discovery and unexpected surprises; it was also a day of returning memories and varying emotions. I had started to retrace my once forgotten childhood steps, recall my past, gaze at tangible evidence of my Cuban life and find the memories, peace, and closures I had come to Cuba looking for. Tonight, relaxing with my friends and enjoying the music of my cultural heritage was exactly what I needed.

It was definitely time to unwind.

Running around Havana all day without lunch had left George, José and me somewhat tired and very hungry. After a rejuvenating Cuban meal at the lavish Club Parisien, my friends and I downed our fair share of Havana Club rum while moving and dancing to the sounds of vintage 1950s Cuban music performed by a cast of world-class musicians, singers, and dancers commemorating the Cuban soundtracks of my life.

It was a fitting way to celebrate a most rewarding and emotional first day back in the country of my birth.

Finally, around two in the morning, the club's general-purpose lights came on, signaling it was time for all patrons, including us, to call it a night.

Sometime later, back in my room and alone with my thoughts, I called my wife Pam and excitedly gave her a report on my first day back in Havana.

"Baby," I concluded, "even if nothing else on this trip goes as well as today, I would leave Cuba satisfied."

She simply responded with a sleepy "I love you."

After such an eventful first day, that was all I needed to hear.

DAY 2

I WAS HIM; HE WAS MY YOUTH

A Most Promising Day

This morning, I wanted to visit the gravesites holding the remains of the loved ones I left behind fifty-six years ago, never to see again. I sought to pray at the foot of my grandparents', uncle's, and aunt's tomb; sense their presence beside me once more; honor their memory; and symbolically reunite our family for the first time since my parents, brother, and I immigrated to the United States in 1960. I also wanted to visit the house I mostly associated with my life in Cuba and walk on the faded footprints of my childhood there. Even though today promised to be one of the most intense days of my journey, I was prepared to withstand the emotional storm that surely awaited me. I needed to continue my search for the memories, inner peace, and closures I came to Cuba looking for.

Today held no guarantees. I knew my Cuban family was buried in Havana's famed Colón Cemetery; I just didn't know where. I also knew that in a 140-acre cemetery with over three hundred thousand graves, it would be difficult enough to find a gravesite location you knew, let alone one you did not. Likewise, the search for Cervantes Street and my Sevillano home could end up in frustrating failure, like yesterday. I chose to concentrate, however, on the joys, experiences, and closures today promised to bring.

I sensed my second day in Havana was going to challenge me, but somehow I knew it would all turn out fine.

George, José, and I met in the hotel restaurant this morning, and after feasting on eggs, tropical fruit, and lots of Cuban coffee, we were ready to start our day.

Maidel arrived to pick us up under the Hotel Nacional's porte cochere and motioned for us to join him. My friends and I squeezed into his car, lowered the windows, and soon found ourselves enjoying the sights and sounds of central Havana on our way to Colón Cemetery.

A few minutes later, we were there.

Finding Our Loved Ones

(May, 2016) Colon Cemetery's monumental gateway

I bought two bouquets of roses from a flower vendor directly outside the cemetery's perimeter walls and placed them inside our car's trunk, next to an envelope I brought from home containing several photographs of my family members living in the United States. I sought to ceremonially place the flowers and photos of my American family on top of the gravesites holding the remains of my Cuban loved ones buried here, thusly reuniting our family for the first time in fifty-six years—even if only through the use of inanimate pictures.

Maidel drove us through Colón Cemetery's magnificent monumental gateway, parked the car next to the main office building, and led us inside the records room.

Once there, he introduced us to the records clerk and asked her to help us locate the addresses of the gravesites my friends and I hoped to visit today. I handed the pretty clerk a handwritten list with the names and dates of death of our family members interred here and watched her disappear with it inside Colón's ancient records vault. Twenty agonizing minutes later, the records clerk walked out of the vault, smiled, waved, and asked me to join her at her desk.

I picked up the nearest available chair, placed it in front of her, and sat down to hear the results of her search.

"I found the addresses of your friends' grandparents and your paternal grandfather's graves," she said. "I did not, however, find an address for your maternal grandfather, Marcos Mateo Marrero's gravesite. Could it possibly be listed under a different name?"

I momentarily froze. Reuniting with the family members I once left behind never to see again, even if only at the foot of their gravesites, was one of the primary reasons I had come to Cuba. I wanted them to know I never forgot them. I needed to tell them how much I always loved them.

I slowed my mind down and started searching within me for something, anything, that might help the records clerk find my Mateo family's gravesite address. Fortunately, I remembered how my cousin Oscar once told me that my maternal grandparents, Marcos and Isaura Mateo, uncle Miguel, and his wife Ileana, were buried in a gravesite listed under Ileana's maiden name, Gimenez Odio. I scribbled the names of the few Gimenez Odio family members I could recall this morning on a piece of paper, handed them to the records clerk, and asked her to please search the cemetery's vault again for any address or telephone numbers listed under those names.

Yes, That Castro

The clerk graciously carried my handwritten names back into the ancient cemetery's vault once more and disappeared from view. I sat back on my rickety wooden chair, still in front of her desk, and hoped for the best. Fifteen minutes later, she returned with information I could have never imagined.

"I am sorry to tell you that we do not have a property or telephone number listed under the names Gimenez or Odio," the clerk informed me.

"Oh no," I responded with a heavy heart. "Are you sure?"

"I do, however, have a phone number associated with a Mateo gravesite listed under a different name," she announced.

"Thank you," I said. "Please give me the number."

The clerk became suddenly solemn, led me toward a quiet corner of the cemetery's lobby, and trying hard not to be overheard, whispered, "I will, but there is something you need to know first. The phone number is listed to Jorge Angel Castro, Fidel Castro's son."

Now THAT I was not expecting!

With much to gain and nothing to lose, I walked outside the records room looking for a private area to make this most unanticipated call and dialed Castro's phone number. To my surprise, Jorge answered on the second ring with a friendly and gentle voice. I greeted him, thanked him for taking my call, and identified myself as Mario Cartaya Mateo.

"Are you related to Miguel Mateo?" he asked.

"Yes," I responded, "I am his nephew."

"Mayito," Castro's son said, "don't you remember me?"

I did not know what to think. Fidel Castro's son had answered my unannounced phone call and knew who I was. Was I supposed to know him too?

"You left Cuba many years ago, didn't you?" he continued.

"Yes, I left in 1960," I said.

"What are you doing back in Cuba?" he wanted to know.

"I am the first of my family in the United States to visit Cuba since we left," I said. "I am at Colón Cemetery trying to find my family's gravesite so I can honor their memory."

"It is so honorable of you to remember your family this way," Castro replied. "How long will you be in Havana?"

"Three more days," I answered.

I asked Jorge Castro how he knew me. He told me we had met when I attended my uncle Miguel's wedding to his ex-wife's aunt, Ileana Gimenez Odio. We would also see each other from time to time, he said, at family celebrations and school events.

"I remember you now," I said, "thank you."

"Have you visited your Mateo family gravesite yet?" Castro asked.

"No," I responded, "the only information the cemetery's records office has of their gravesite address is your phone listing. That's how I got your number. Do you know the location of the gravesite?"

"I don't know the location of your family's gravesite, Mayito, but my ex-wife, Ena Lydia, does," Castro said. "We divorced ten years ago, however, and have not spoken to each other since."

"I guess divorces are as messy in Havana as they are in Miami," I responded lightheartedly.

Castro's son laughed and then said, "I really want to help you, Mayito. Here is what I can do: I will call my sister-in-law, Vivian, who lives in Germany, tell her you are in Colón Cemetery looking for your family's gravesite, and ask her to call my ex-wife in Havana for her to reach out to you with your Mateo family's gravesite address as soon as possible."

I knew this complicated chain of events would have to rely on the successful completion of multiple international calls using Cuba's antiquated telephone infrastructure, Vivian and Ena Lydia promptly answering their phones, and their willingness to help an estranged ex-husband as well as a family member they had not heard from in fifty-six years. I prepared myself for the worst—but hoped for the best once more.

"Thank you for all your help," I said.

"It is my pleasure to help you, Mayito," Castro replied.

"Perhaps if things had turned out differently, you and I could have been close family friends," I mused.

"I would have liked that," he wistfully assured me.

I gave him Maidel's cell phone number for Ena Lydia to call, said goodbye, and started walking toward our black Chinese sedan.

I wondered how different our lives would have been without the rise of his father's revolution.

The Plan

A couple of minutes later, I arrived at the car and joined my friends, already deep in conversation about how to best approach our visit to the cemetery today. I suggested that Maidel should take us to my paternal grandfather's gravesite first—since the records clerk had previously mentioned it was the closest to us—followed by the graves holding George's and José's grandparents, before ending our visit to Colón Cemetery at my Mateo family's tomb. This arrangement, I thought, would best allow me the time I needed to receive Ena Lydia's phone call with the gravesite address of my Mateo family while we were still visiting the cemetery today. Everyone agreed.

Now, all we had to do was find the gravesites.

My friends and I climbed into Maidel's car, reviewed the property addresses given to us by the cemetery's records clerk earlier this morning, and immediately realized we were way over our heads. We desperately needed help!

Thankfully, seconds later, the cavalry arrived. One of the several groundskeepers working outside the cemetery's main office building unexpectedly approached our car and tapped on the front passenger door, next to where I sat.

I lowered the car window next to my seat, looked at our profusely sweating visitor, and asked him, "May I help you?'

"Gentlemen," he said, "the Colón Cemetery gravesite layout was designed by the Spanish monks who founded it over a hundred years ago. It is almost impossible to find the location of a gravesite here without help. May I offer you my services as your guide today?"

"Is it really that difficult?" I asked naively.

"Yes," the groundskeeper-wanting-to-be-our-guide explained. "All gravesites in Colón Cemetery are recorded with an address location identified as the number of Spanish monk paces taken toward defined compass directions emanating from the existing quadrant markers located throughout the cemetery. You would never find a gravesite here, but I can. I have been working here for thirty years."

That was all I needed to hear. Since none of us in Maidel's car were Spanish monks, had a compass, knew how long a monk's pace was, or could ever find the cemetery's quadrant markers in this vast cemetery, I asked the moonlighting groundskeeper to join us in our air-conditioned car and become our guide. Negotiating a fair fee for his services was not a problem—he could have had whatever he wanted.

Julio and Isabel

It took approximately twenty minutes for our groundskeeper-turned-guide to find the first quadrant marker, ascertain the inscribed compass direction, and walk the recorded number of nineteenth-century Spanish monk paces leading us to the 1924 gravesite containing the remains of Julio Cartaya, the paternal grandfather I never knew and who died when my father was only four years old.

Surprisingly, Julio's name was not engraved on his crypt; "*Isabel Russo*"—his wife and my paternal grandmother's name was! Sensing my confusion, our moonlighting groundskeeper put his sweaty arm around my shoulder and calmly said, "I know it looks strange, but in Colón Cemetery, it is customary to engrave the names of the property owners on the crypts. The interred are identified on tablets placed above the tombs. I know it's different than what you boys are used to in Miami, but don't worry, it's just the way things are done here."

Discovering my grandfather's tomb was engraved only with my grandmother's name was a most surreal and ironic moment. With her name chiseled on the granite crypt containing her husband's remains and because she long ago decided never to date again or remarry, I was certain my grandmother intended to one day be buried here with him as well. She had no reason to expect otherwise.

The winds of political change, however, would unexpectedly sweep through Cuba in 1959, ushering in a new era incompatible with our continued lives there. A few years after my parents, brother, and I emigrated from Cuba, my grandmother followed us to the United States, leaving her country, crypt, and husband's remains behind.

Forty years ago, we buried her in Miami.

The sad reality of the Cuban Diaspora is that Julio and Isabel, once meant to rest in perpetuity together, are buried in different countries, forever separated by about two hundred miles.

Both burial markers, remarkably enough, will always bear my grandmother's name.

Still contemplating Julio and Isabel's unfortunate fate, I noticed Maidel walking excitedly toward me with his cell phone in hand.

"Mario, I have a phone call for you," Maidel announced as he handed me his cell phone.

The Call I Hoped For

It had only been thirty minutes since my conversation with Jorge Castro, and unbelievably, his ex-wife, Ena Lydia, was already on the phone asking to speak with me.

"Mayito," Ena Lydia exclaimed, "it's so nice to talk with you again."

No one except family members and *old* friends refers to me by my childhood name any longer. I started to wonder how well Ena Lydia knew me.

"It's nice to speak with you as well," I responded.

"Welcome to Cuba," she offered.

"Thank you for calling me back so quickly," I said.

"Do you remember me?" she asked. "I am your aunt Ileana's niece and attended school at Instituto Edison with you. Your mother, Leida, was my kindergarten teacher. How is she?"

"She is a frail ninety-three years old," I responded, "but still has a sharp mind."

"I remember her so lovingly," Ena Lydia continued, "and I remember you too. You used to be good friends with my younger sister, Vivian."

"I remember Vivian," I said. "She once portrayed a doll that came to life while I played an elderly watchmaker in our first-grade school play."

"Yes," she said, "I was there. You were adorable."

During the next half hour, Ena Lydia and I spoke about our families and reminisced about the past. Politics and fate had separated us decades ago. Today, however, we were speaking again, having come full circle.

"We loved your family, Mayito," Ena Lydia continued. "When your grandparents and uncle died, it was our pleasure to bury them with your aunt Ileana next to our family. Walk over there and visit with them."

Ena Lydia then read me my Mateo family's gravesite location coordinates, including the cemetery quadrant, point of compass, and number of Spanish monk paces.

"Ena, I cannot thank you enough," I said.

"Don't be silly," she answered. "We are family."

"Reuniting with my grandparents, uncles, and aunt today," I added, "is going to be a dream come true. Thank you, from the bottom of my heart."

"Go there, Mayito," she concluded, "and finally put your heart at ease."

According to our new guide, the gravesite address Ena Lydia gave me located my Mateo family's crypt on the opposite end of the cemetery from my Cartaya grandfather's crypt. My friends' family gravesites, our next two stops, were conveniently located on the way there. José, George, the sweaty groundskeeper-turned-guide, and I climbed inside Maidel's black sedan and continued the search for our family members' final resting places.

George's Grandmother

George, born in the United States, had never met his grandmother. He was about to introduce himself in front of her gravesite for the first time today. Once we got there, George grew solemn and stared in silence at her crypt. A few minutes later, he wiped tears from his eyes, flashed a smile of satisfaction, placed his arm around my shoulders, and said,

"Brother, these are my Cuban roots."

"George, why are you smiling?" I asked.

"I've never felt so Cuban," he responded.

I understood. He was facing his unresolved past and discovering his personal vault. I hugged him back and whispered, "Welcome home, brother."

José's Grandmother

Ten minutes later, we arrived at the crypt containing the remains of José's grandmother. He remembered little about her, except that she was a high-ranking member of the Santeria religion (a secretive Afro-Cuban faith tracing its roots to West African slaves). Our groundskeeper-turned-guide, also a devotee of the faith, immediately recognized José's grandmother as having been a well-known Cuban high priestess of the cult.

The markings and offerings on her gravesite further confirmed it.

To honor her, our groundskeeper-turned-guide-now turned Santeria singer, impulsively performed a religious ritual at the foot of her grave spoken in Lucumí, the Santeria language of the occult. None of us had ever seen or heard anything like this before.

George and I were a little uncomfortable at first. We did not understand the ritual or language spoken. Eventually, however, we grew to appreciate watching a secretive and dramatic religious ceremony, very much a part of Cuban folklore, few nonbelievers ever see. Watching José smile as the ceremony unfolded made it all worthwhile.

When the impromptu gravesite Santeria ceremony ended, José thanked the sweaty groundskeeper-turned-guide-turned-Santeria-singer, looked at us, and said, "Guys, this was the real thing."

Not that it was ever in doubt!

Successfully Reuniting My Family

With that, we got back inside Maidel's car and headed toward the gravesite containing the remains of the Mateo family members I left behind fifty-six years ago, never to see again. I could hardly believe I was about to achieve the reunion I had always dreamed of but often feared would never happen. I spent the interminable drive to their gravesite fighting back the tears that wanted to appear with a forced and ungenuine smile.

A few minutes later, we arrived at their gravesite. I was now the first member of my family in the United States to visit my maternal family at the foot of their graves in Cuba. My dream of a family reunion was incredibly just moments away from becoming reality.

I wiped the sad smile off my face, hugged my friends, and rejoiced at the significance of the moment. I could not believe that after such a lengthy and emotional family separation I was finally here, carrying with me the love of my deceased father and brother, the heart of my frail and elderly mother, and the promise of the family I built and shared a life with in the United States.

I stared at my Mateo family's grave in thankful disbelief; the remains of the loved ones I grew up living with and had not seen for five decades were just inches away from me now.

I thought about the slow deterioration and eventual deaths of my Mateo family members in Havana while my parents, brother, and I struggled to communicate with them from Miami. It was a time of heightened separation anxiety, deep sorrow, and great suffering for my family members in the United States and Cuba alike.

The old painful feelings of impotence resulting from the cruel, inhuman, and punishing USA-Cuba travel and communication restrictions of the 1960s had unforgivingly returned to haunt my spirits again this morning at Colón Cemetery.

Some wounds, I realized, are just slow to heal.

I asked George, José, Maidel, and our sweaty groundskeeper-turned-guide to wait for me in the car. I needed a few private moments to gather my thoughts and come to grips with my emerging emotions.

I kneeled in front of my Mateo family's gravesite and prayed for my grandparents', uncle's, and aunt's souls. I told them how I wished I could have been with them during their final days, how much I always loved them and how I had continually strived to keep their memory alive. I told them my wife and I named our son, Mario Marcos, after my grandfather and our daughter named her son, Angel Mateo, in honor of our family's surname. I promised them that their legacy would continue to live in our love and stories as well as our children's and grandchildren's names.

I told them how I missed them every day since we separated and wished things would have turned out differently.

Still kneeling at the foot of my Mateo family's gravesite this morning, I recalled how my grandfather was the first of my Cuban loved ones to pass on. During his lengthy illness and eventual death in Havana, my father asked me to be strong for my grieving mother in Miami by avoiding any outward display of emotions. At the age of fifteen, I buried the pain of losing the grandfather I lived with during the first nine years of my life—and loved as a second father—inside the same protective subconscious vault I had already built to shelter me from the anguish of family separation and struggles of my early years in exile.

After my grandfather's passing, it became easier to bury the distress, misery, and feelings of ineptness from each of my remaining family members' illnesses and deaths in Cuba inside the same vault.

I never disappointed my father; through it all, I never cried.

This morning, all that would change. The trauma and pain associated with our family's separation and the deaths of my loved ones buried inside the lifeless crypt now in front of me, bubbled to the surface with an intensity and sorrow that caught me by surprise. The tears of fifty-six years finally appeared, allowing me to sob a prolonged release of raw and cleansing emotions long overdue. I prayed and cried at the foot of my family's grave in recurrent waves of emotions for several more minutes.

I had finally allowed myself to grieve.

Once I placed the bouquet of roses on top of my Mateo family's crypt and safely slid the photographs of my loved ones living in the United States inside its marble tablet's sleeve, I had successfully reunited our one family—even if only symbolically—for the first time since my parents, brother, and I fled Cuba fifty-six years ago. My dreams of the family reunification I once feared might never happen had incredibly come true.

I wished my parents and brother could have been here to share this moment with me today.

Then the most curious thing happened. Standing next to my family's crypt, still staring at the photographs I had just placed inside its marble tablet, my mind wandered back to a typical Sunday in our Apolo home. I could see and hear my father and uncles telling jokes and drinking beer on the front porch, my grandmother serving lunch on our dining room table, and my mother playing Lecuona compositions on the piano while my grandfather kept an eye over the entire scene.

The loving bond that once defined our family had somehow found me again today, in front of their final resting place.

A smile emerged out of my tears and, for a fleeting and beautiful moment, my entire family surrounded me once more.

Finally at peace with myself, I grew thankful and truly happy. I had my closure.

(May, 2016) Symbolically reuniting my family in Colon Cemetery

Oxygen, Lunch, Baseball, and a Toast of Hope

After such an emotional morning, my friends and I needed a place to lighten the mood. Maidel recommended the *Paladar San*

Cristobal as the perfect place to go have lunch. He told us the food there was delicious, the waiters were friendly, and its walls were covered with hundreds of Cuban paraphernalia from the 1950s, including pre-Castro era posters and vintage photographs from my childhood days here. He was sure it would make us feel at home. The *San Cristobal* was also the restaurant, he informed us, where President Obama had lunch during his recent historic visit to Havana.

If this place was good enough for our president, I thought, then it was definitely good enough for us.

Maidel, George, José, and I arrived at the *San Cristobal* a few minutes after noon and were met by a rather large photograph of President Obama in the restaurant's lobby. It made us smile. A uniformed waiter greeted us, led us to our table, and immediately started to share his cell phone pictures proudly posing with the American president during his recent visit for lunch here. Within minutes, we were joined by several of his co-workers wanting to show off their photographs with President Obama as well. We all started to laugh.

Our waiter, still laughing, told us how hopeful they all were for the future of Cuba. The reason, he said, was because they had "oxygen" now. "Having oxygen," he explained, referred to the American president's speech at the *Gran Teatro de la Habana* and his message that the future of Cuba belonged to Cuba's youth. President Obama's visit to Havana earlier this year, our waiter explained, had a large impact on all Cubans throughout the island.

My friends and I ordered a round of cold beer, continued laughing with our new American President-loving friends, and proceeded to order lunch.

Minutes later, after finishing my delicious Cuban meal, I decided to stretch my legs and look at some of the baseball paraphernalia neatly displayed on the walls of the restaurant while I waited for the cups of Cuban coffee my friends and I had already ordered to arrive at our table. Just a few steps into my walk, however, one of the other guests in the restaurant that day approached me wanting to talk about the Almendares baseball team—whose vintage 1950s cap I was wearing. After our spontaneous, but nonetheless spirited baseball conversation came to an end, my new friend introduced himself as Raul, smiled, and asked me to follow him into a private section of the restaurant with several photographs of the 1958 Havana baseball team—Almendares' archrival—hanging on its walls.

Once there, he mischievously claimed that Havana, his favorite team, would always defeat my Almendares team. I disagreed, of course, starting a good-natured discussion he admitted not to have enjoyed for over thirty years—neither had I.

Hardly anyone in Cuba today remembers much from the prerevolution Cuban Professional Baseball League. I had found the rare person who did. It was fun!

I shook Raul's hand, waved goodbye, and rejoined my friends at our table just in time to drink my Cuban coffee.

Our uniformed waiter and his co-workers surprised us by bringing complimentary shot glasses of Havana Club rum to our table, wanting a toast with us to *El Cambio* (Cuban reforms). We toasted with our delicious drinks of hope and bonded with our new friends in a moment of Cuban brotherhood.

It was a beautiful way to end a perfect morning.

Maidel was right; the *Paladar San Cristobal* was exactly what we needed to brighten the day. The waiters were friendly, the food was delicious, memories of Cuba's baseball glory days surrounded us, and the island's new "oxygen" of hope filled the air we breathed.

This afternoon, with our stomachs full of Cuban food and a second wind powered by good rum and Cuban coffee, my friends and I decided to attempt finding my Sevillano home again. We waved goodbye to our new Cuban friends, took selfies posing with Obama's photograph in the restaurant's lobby, left the *Paladar San Cristobal,* and started our drive through the streets of Havana in search of the address we could not find yesterday.

Today, however, Maidel was bringing a GPS device he borrowed from a friend last night to help us find the elusive Cervantes Street. The odds of finding my Sevillano home were much improved.

Finding My Elusive Sevillano Home

I lived in my Sevillano home from the ages of five to eight years old. It was the place where I spent my most formative years in Cuba and mostly associated with my childhood in Havana. My excitement grew with every street we passed on our drive there. I couldn't wait to see it again.

This afternoon, with a little help from his friend's GPS device, Maidel found Cervantes Street and started counting down the posted house numbers searching for a house located at Cervantes 90½. He drove past Cervantes 96, Cervantes 94, and Cervantes 92. Next to Cervantes 92 there was an empty lot, immediately followed by Cervantes 88. The vacant lot, I thought, was probably the property where my former home once stood.

Heartsick, I informed Maidel that my Sevillano house had apparently not survived the years and we should leave. The search for my most memorable home in Cuba, I feared, was surely over—I would have to come to grips with my disappointment.

Maidel parked the black Chinese sedan in front of the empty lot, looked at me, and said, "Mario, don't give up hope. No one ever demolishes a house in Havana. Continue looking around. It's got to be around here somewhere."

Then out of the corner of my eye, I noticed a man smoking a cigarette on the balcony of the house directly across from us, staring at our official-looking black sedan with the dark-tinted windows as if we were his most dubious strangers for the day.

Undaunted, I stepped out of Maidel's car, took a deep breath of hope, and started walking toward him.

"Good afternoon," I said.

"Yes," the cigarette-smoking neighbor responded, nervous and aloof at the sight of a most dubious stranger wanting to speak with him.

"Was there ever a house on that empty lot across the street?" I asked, pointing to it.

"No," he responded. "I have lived here for almost sixty years, and there has never been a house on that lot. Why do you want to know?"

That was the answer I was hoping to hear! I had arrived at Cervantes Street with all the dreams and excitement of a child returning home and dreaded the thought of leaving Havana without bonding with the childhood years I once spent there. A siren song and a serious dose of good luck had led me this far; now was the time to complete finding my way back. I had many unanswered questions and faded memories to reclaim from my former Sevillano home.

I cleared my throat, smiled, and continued our conversation. "I'm looking for the house where I grew up near here," I said.

"What is your name?" he asked, still puffing on his cigarette.

"Mario Cartaya Mateo," I responded.

He thought for a moment, smiled, and said, "There used to be a Mateo that lived on this side of the street just a few houses away, but that was a long time ago. You are looking on the wrong side of the road. Walk in that direction," he pointed, "and you will find what you are looking for. Good luck brother."

"Thank you," I uttered with great humility and gratitude.

I stared at the stranger and wondered if I had ever played with him as a child. In my excitement to find my family's Sevillano home, however, I forgot to ask him.

Luck had smiled upon me again. I was granted a second chance. With a sudden source of energy and renewed resolve, I started walking blindly along the middle of Cervantes Street looking for a home I had not seen (even in photographs) since 1959.

I did not have to walk far. The cigarette-smoking neighbor was right—the home where I lived my most memorable years in Cuba was on his side of the street, barely a few houses away. It didn't take long for me to find it.

I told myself everything was fine and started to approach my former Sevillano home.

The beautiful two-story Spanish-style house that once filled my life with so much joy and childhood wonder looked exactly the way I always imagined it. The only difference was that its street address was 70½ Cervantes Street (not 90½, as I previously thought).

My friends and I walked on the sidewalk past the property's perimeter fence, entered my former home's front yard through an unlocked gate, and knocked on the elegant textured glass and decorative steel-frame front door I suddenly remembered so well.

An Inauspicious Curveball

Waiting for someone to answer the door, my mind wandered back to the day, long ago, when I played on the entry porch of this house pretending to be Almendares pitcher Orlando Peña. Peña had a wicked curveball, and I wanted to pitch just like him. Over and over again, against my grandmother's objections, I practiced throwing my curveball against the stucco-finished wall next to our beautiful—and suddenly vulnerable—glazed front door.

My father arrived home from work early that day and parked his car alongside the street curb. Being seven years old and wanting to impress him with my newly refined baseball skills, I yelled out, "Papi, look at my curveball. I have been practicing it. Watch me!"

I went into my windup, just like Orlando Peña used to, and released the ball as hard as I could. Unfortunately, the pitch did not go where I aimed it. My father and I watched in horror as the ball missed the stucco wall but not the textured glass and decorative steel front door my family was so proud of.

My inauspicious curveball sailed through the door's textured glass that day, shattering it into uncountable little pieces, immediately covering the ground upon which I stood frozen in place. With nowhere for me to hide, I started to cry with a mixture of adolescent embarrassment and athletic shame typical of my young age, screaming over and over again, "This could only happen to me!"

Then the most amazing thing happened. My father did not yell, scold, or even send me to my room for solitary confinement. He simply lifted me off the ground, hugged me, and said, "Mayito, we need to work on that curveball, but first we need to replace the glass."

(May, 2016) The Sevillano home's decorative front door with the textured glass I once shattered with a really bad curve ball.

Inside My Sevillano Home

This afternoon, fifty-eight years after that horrific pitch, a man opened the same decorative steel front door (with the replacement textured glass my father and I once installed) from inside the house and stared at my friends and me in obvious distrust.

With much to gain and little to lose, I smiled and introduced myself, "Hello, my name is Mario Cartaya Mateo. I used to live in this house during the mid-1950s."

The man relaxed his expression, smiled back at me, and said, "I am Gilberto Fernandez. My mother bought this house immediately after your family moved out. I remember your last name."

"Would you be so kind to allow my friends and me inside your home?" I asked. "There are so many things I want to remember from my time living here."

"Of course," he responded, "just don't go into any of the upstairs bedrooms. My mother is up there taking a nap, and she's in a bad mood."

I was disappointed; the bedroom that formed the background for two of my most memorable moments from my life in Cuba was on the second floor of this house. This was the room my father "smuggled" me out of, even though I was sick with a fever, so we could attend the Cuban Sugar Kings' 1959 Triple-A Baseball Championship Game in Cerro Stadium—an unforgettable night of championship dreams, baseball heroes, and father-son bonds. This was also the bedroom where my grandfather woke me up one New Year's morning with the news that Castro's rebels had won their insurrection and would soon be in Havana—a historical event that forever altered the trajectory of my family's life.

It would have been great to visit and stand inside the bedroom that meant so much to me once more. Too bad Gilberto's mother was in a bad mood!

"Follow me," Gilberto said and led my friends and me inside his home.

I was finally inside the home I mostly associated with my Cuban childhood—it felt like a dream come true! For many years, I had struggled with the strange sensation that something from inside its walls was calling me back. Today, I needed to discover the source of my Sevillano home's siren song.

Not knowing what to make of my developing emotions, I grew solemn and withdrew to the quiet place I often go in search of solace and understanding. Gilberto, seemingly sensing my suddenly introspective mood, looked at me, smiled again, and offered to take my friends and me on a tour of his home.

It did not take long before childhood memories from when I lived in my Sevillano home started to return. At first, they revealed themselves as a trickle of black-and-white still photographs continuously gaining in speed, momentum, and volume until eventually evolving into the long-forgotten Technicolor movie reels of my life, beautifully awash with the emotions, context, and sounds that once defined my days growing up here. It made me glad to be back home.

I stared at the large horizontal living room windows and wistfully recalled how my family always placed our decorated Christmas trees in front of them. Gifts from Santa Claus and the Three Wise Men would magically appear here every year.

I imagined the voices and laughter of the loved ones I once lived with in this house, encouraging me to open my presents. I smiled at the memory of one very special Christmas Day when I unwrapped my ultimate Christmas wish: a blue-and-white Almendares baseball team uniform, complete with a baseball cap and blue stirrups.

For a brief Christmas moment in May, my parents, grandparents, nanny, uncles, and aunts were with me in this room once more—even if only in my mind.

Gilberto opened the door leading into a room I recognized as our old study room, where my grandfather once took great pride tutoring my brother and me in subjects way beyond our school's already-ambitious curriculum. Inside this room, I blossomed academically and artistically under his loving, educated, and patient guidance, forming the foundations of my love for architecture, mathematics, and art. Here, my grandfather and I built a bond that never tarnished, outlasting fifty years of the Cuban Diaspora and his untimely death.

I missed my grandfather again.

A few steps later, Gilberto opened another door leading into what was once my uncle Miguel's forbidden bachelor's bedroom—it made me smile.

"Why are you smiling that way?" Gilberto asked.

"This was a room I was never allowed to go in," I awkwardly responded.

"Why?" he wanted to know.

"Because this was my bachelor uncle Miguel's bedroom," I explained.

"So you have never been inside this room?" he asked again.

"Oh no," I said, "I have definitely been here before. One day I sneaked in and found his *Playboy* magazine collection inside one of his drawers."

"Did you look at them?" Gilberto solicited with a mischievous grin.

"What was a seven-year-old boy supposed to do?" I said. "Of course, I looked at them. I still remember how upset my grandfather became when he caught me red-handed gawking at a centerfold picture of a naked Playboy bunny."

"Did you get in trouble?" Gilberto asked while laughing hysterically.

"Oh yeah, my curiosity that day earned me a most embarrassing lecture by my usually doting grandfather and a lengthy in-bedroom incarceration from my perplexed mother," I informed him. "I did not mind though. I had seen my first pictures of a woman's breasts. It was truly a day I will never forget."

"Mario, you still haven't changed," José said, and everyone started to laugh.

We left my uncle Miguel's bedroom and walked toward the garage. Once there, I remembered the day I sat on a wooden stool talking with my grandfather as he worked on one of his many carpentry projects, drenched in the sweat of Havana's midday summer heat. I asked him to stop working for a moment that day, sighed, and with all the innocence of my young years, told him, "Tata, I feel a funny flutter in my heart watching you work so hard."

My grandfather smiled, stopped what he was doing, stepped out from behind his workbench, hugged me, and tenderly said, "Mayito, you have given me a great gift. That flutter you feel in your heart means you love me. I feel the same flutter for you, son. I love you too."

So this, I remembered thinking that beautiful day long ago, *is what love feels like.*

Today, I was fortunate to return to the spot on earth where, at the tender age of six, I first learned the feeling of love. For a brief instant, my heart remembered the pure, unconditional, and innocent love it once felt as a small child in this garage. It was wonderful to feel that beautiful moment once more.

Gilberto then opened a door leading to my former home's spacious backyard, conjuring lighthearted images of the many unscripted games I once played with my family and friends there.

I thought about how pure and innocent my life was during that time. I also thought about how my friends and I would sometimes chase after a rooster and chicken, named Napoleon and Josephine, my grandfather kept as pets inside a chicken coop tucked in the far corner of the yard—until the adults made us stop.

One fateful morning for Josephine, my grandfather discovered her lifeless inside the coop; by nightfall, she had become our main dinner entrée. Once I joined my family for dinner that night, and my brother told me whom we were being served, I refused to eat.

My parents and grandparents just smiled and made me a ham-and-cheese sandwich.

Once Napoleon died, my father made sure we never had chickens or roosters as pets again.

George, José, and I left the backyard, followed Gilberto into his living room, and started to talk about our lives and families. We shared stories, laughed, and drank cold soft drinks in an effort to keep cool inside his unair-conditioned room. It was a welcomed moment of levity, especially considering what would happen next.

A few minutes later, with Gilberto's permission, I left the living room conversation, walked toward the adjacent modernist marble stairway, and fearlessly climbed the steps leading to the second-floor balcony. That was as far as Gilberto would allow me to go; the second-floor bedrooms where my family and I once slept were still off-limits.

I dared not go there anyways—his mother was in her bedroom taking a nap, and she was in a bad mood!

The Night that Changed My Life

I reached the top of my former home's modernist stairway, sat on the floor behind the second-floor balcony railing balustrades, and stared at the living room below, where Gilberto and my friends were still busy talking and drinking cold soda.

I remembered how fifty-seven years ago, my parents, grandparents, uncles, and aunts gathered in the same living room now below me amid great sorrow and confusion. My father, whose whereabouts during the previous twenty-four hours had been unknown, was finally back home after being detained and warned by Cuba's revolutionary militia that, as a result of his refusal to cooperate with their American property nationalization efforts, his future safety in Cuba was no longer guaranteed. There was a sense of heightened concern on the faces of my loved ones as they sat grim and solemn waiting for my father to speak that night. Everyone feared that going forward, he could "disappear" at any time.

In an effort to shield my brother and me from the sad events about to unfold in the living room, my father sent us upstairs to bed early.

My brother promptly obeyed him—I did not.

This afternoon I found myself once again sitting behind the same second-floor balcony railing balustrades from where I once peeked at the sad events unfolding below me that night, long ago. I remembered watching my father walk toward the center of the living room and, with his voice cracking from emotion, ask my extended family for permission to leave Cuba with my mother, brother, and me toward an uncertain life of exile in the United States.

Everyone in the living room below me groaned and started to cry that dreadful night. Alone and confused in the balcony above them, I wept as well.

After all the sobbing finally stopped, my grandfather walked up to my father, put an arm around his broad shoulders, and calmly said, "Ignacio, you cannot be a husband to my daughter and a father to my grandchildren if you are dead. Travel to America with your family and return to us when it's safe again."

Our lives would never be the same again.

Finding the Siren Song Within Me

Today, fifty-seven years after that life-changing event, I was back in my Sevillano home sitting on the very same spot from where I first learned, at the tender age of eight, that my time living in Cuba was coming to an end. Memories of my Cuban life before that consequential night—and the American life that followed—started to oscillate indiscriminately between the two this afternoon, continuously gaining in speed until astonishingly culminating in a most surreal vision of my eight-year-old self sitting beside me.

I stared at this most unusual sight and tried to understand the meaning of the moment thrust upon me. His innocent demeanor and youthful wonder surprised me. The ills of the world seemed years away from affecting him. He could not, I thought, understand the future that awaited him—he was too young and naive.

I, in turn, did know the scars he would develop and the protective subconscious vault he would eventually have to build along the way. At first, I wanted to protect him from all that but quickly realized I wouldn't have to.

I had already done that for both of us.

It was his voice, I now understood, that for years had called me back to my Sevillano home, seeking his release from the protective subconscious vault I once discarded him to during our metamorphosis into an American. We were not meeting here by chance today; he was the siren song that brought me back.

He had been waiting a lifetime for this moment—so had I.

We sat next to each other on the only spot on earth where this improbable moment was possible, staring into a most unusual mirror displaying not our individual reflections but our singular image instead. For years, we had been but one torn in two, aching to be mended. I embraced the vision of my eight-year-old Cuban childhood behind the very same Sevillano home second-floor balcony railing balustrades from where we once separated and cried the tears of a lifetime divided until he was gone.

Safely within my consciousness, never to be forgotten again, my eight-year-old self and I merged as one once more—our disparate Cuban and American stories forever reunited as our one unique life.

I remained sitting alone behind those old railing balusters a little longer, simultaneously crying and smiling at the intensity, beauty, and meaning of this most incredible moment. Once my tears dried, I returned downstairs and joined Gilberto and my friends in the living room. They looked curiously at me and my tear-swollen eyes but said nothing—neither did I.

By now, however, the afternoon had already started to turn into the early evening hours, and it was time to leave my Sevillano home toward our next destination. My friends and

Gilberto stood up from their living room chairs and met me next to the beautiful decorative steel and textured glass front door I once shattered with my inauspicious curveball.

I couldn't help but smile again—I realized I never did learn how to throw a curveball like Orlando Peña!

Gilberto opened the front door for us to leave, looked down at his feet, put on a brave smile, and sadly affirmed, "Mario, now you get to go back to Miami, but unfortunately, I have to stay behind in this land of constant struggles."

It was difficult to see Gilberto so resigned to the hopelessness of his future in Cuba. George, José, Maidel, and I had established a friendly relationship with him today, and it was hard saying goodbye. We hugged him, thanked him for his hospitality, promised to stay in touch, and walked out the front door toward our car.

Luckily, there were no pieces of shattered glass from the still beautiful decorative steel and textured glass front door for us to walk over this afternoon.

(May, 2016) Gilberto and me outside my former Sevillano house

The Soil of My Birth

My friends and I settled inside Maidel's car, waved goodbye to Gilberto, and started our drive toward the place where I was born, the former *Quinta de Dependientes* Hospital (now known as *La Purisima*).

I remembered family stories describing how my six-foot-four-inch-tall uncle Marcolin arrived at this hospital after visiting hours on the day of my birth. Undeterred by being denied visiting rights because of the late hour, he still somehow managed to sneak his tall frame inside the Romagosa Maternity Pavillion's corridor and started looking through the glass transoms above the doors of every patient room until he found ours—scaring the nurses half to death along the way.

Moments later, my friends and I arrived at the hospital and, with the help of one of the nurses, found its former maternity hall, still defined by the vintage decorative wood patient room doors with the glass transoms above. With every click of my camera's shutter, I could not help but smile at the thought of my mischievous uncle's visit to my mother's maternity room on the day I was born.

It was hard to believe I was taking photographs of the very spot on earth where I took my first breath.

I missed my uncle Marcolin today.

"Life is best lived with a
never ending thirst for exploration."
Marcolin

(May, 2016) Romagosa Maternity Pavillion—the place of my birth
Former Quinta de Dependientes Hospital

Aragon, Benny, Lecuona, and Smiles

We left the hospital and rushed back to the Hotel Nacional wanting to shower, dress, and make our presence known at another of Havana's famed nightclubs.

Tonight, my friends and I sought a fun place to celebrate a most eventful and emotional day in Cuba. Still full from our large Cuban lunch at the *Paladar San Cristobal*, we decided to skip dinner and go see the show at the Hotel Nacional's famed Salon 1930.

During the 1930s through 1950s, this lavish cabaret attracted thousands of visitors to watch the greatest American and international performers of the era. Today, it attracted George, José, and me to see a performance of the cabaret's band with two former members of the Buena Vista Social Club, one of Cuba's renowned contemporary groups.

The show lasted a little over two hours and featured Cuban pop music from the 1940s and 1950s, including the music of the Orquesta Aragón, Benny Moré, and other Cuban performers of the era. During band breaks, a featured pianist played Lecuona compositions, reminding me of my mother—who loved playing his music on her piano.

I missed my mother tonight.

(Circa 1970) My mother and her piano

Tonight, Salon 1930 felt and sounded like the Cuba I grew up in. After the show ended, my friends and I remained at the club for the postshow party and continued to celebrate the end of a most improbable day—toasting to our friendship with each glass of Havana Club we consumed, dancing to express the fountain of emotions pouring out of our hearts, and basking in the feelings of joy that filled us with unabashed happiness. Today, after all, had been another incredible day of discoveries, surprises, returning memories, and profound feelings of love and wonder.

Unfortunately, the time of night eventually arrived when, tired and needing rest, we decided to call it a night.

It was time to go back to our rooms.

Lying awake in bed in the predawn hours of the morning, I wondered what effect my astonishing experiences today would have on the rest of my life. I hoped they would make me a better version of myself.

A sense of complete calm finally overwhelmed me, and I drifted into sleep with a song from the Cabaret's show in my mind, a reunited life, peace in my heart, and a smile on my face.

DAY 3

"IT REMINDS US OF ALL THAT ONCE WAS GOOD, AND IT COULD BE AGAIN"

— Field of Dreams

The Cuban Sun

I woke up this morning wearing the same silly smile I fell asleep with last night. Still only daybreak, the morning Cuban sun was already shining through the half-closed wooden slat window shades, sending its warm beams of daylight dancing alternatively between the walls and ceiling of my hotel room.

It was a great way to start the day.

Today, I hoped that visiting the buildings, parks, and plazas that once formed the background of my life in Cuba would help me continue to recall the forgotten Cuban childhood memories I sought to find. I also wanted to rediscover the cultural heritage and patrimony of my birthright.

I knew outside my room the sun was already illuminating Havana's sights. Soon, I hoped, it would shine on me as well.

An Opportunistic Plaza

After breakfast this morning, my friends and I sat in the Hotel Nacional's opulent lobby and waited for Maidel to come pick us up. Minutes later, he arrived and joined us to discuss the day's itinerary.

It was good to see Maidel this morning. My friends and I were ready and anxious to start the day.

We walked out of the hotel, climbed into the black Chinese sedan with the dark-tinted windows, and started our drive toward the famed *Plaza de la Revolución*—our first stop today.

Once there, the reality and contradictions intrinsic to this magnificent public square surprised us. The place where Fidel Castro delivered his often hours-long anti-American tirades was, ironically, also the holy ground where Pope John Paul II, Pope Benedict XVI, and Pope Francis held large catholic services and prayed for an end to the Cuban Revolution's once systematic suppression of religious worship on the island.

Paradoxically, the Cuban Revolution's defining square— capable of hosting up to a million visitors at a time—was, in reality, the former *Plaza Civica* and surrounding government buildings built years prior to Castro's rise to power, now rebranded as the official forum of Castro's revolution.

I remembered this place well; I had been here before. Other than the steel portraits and quotations from Cuban revolutionary heroes Che Guevara and Camilo Cienfuegos strategically mounted on the facades of two buildings defining this square, not much had changed in this plaza since the last time I saw it in 1960.

Guevara's and Cienfuegos's steel portraits and quotations on display here are, however, historically irreconcilable with their revolutionary legacies. Che Guevara was Argentinian, not Cuban. His time fighting alongside Fidel Castro served to redefine him as a rebel seeking hemispheric communist insurrection through violence. Soon after leaving Cuba, the emboldened Guevara was killed in Bolivia attempting a South American insurgency that never materialized. The quote under his steel portrait, "*Hasta la victoria siempre*" (Until victory forever), is incompatible with his eventual failure, capture, and death. Camilo Cienfuegos was a Cuban who fought alongside Fidel Castro as well. The quotation under his portrait, "*Vas bien Fidel*" (You are doing fine, Fidel), was from the early days after the triumph of the revolution. Months later, Cienfuegos grew unhappy with the government's cruelty, left Havana to live in the city of Camagüey, and began to challenge Castro's evolving political policies. Unhappy with Cienfuegos's defiance, the Cuban leader summoned him back to Havana in order to discuss their differences. We might never know the truth surrounding his death, but many historians still suspect the disappearance of his small engine plane as he flew from Camagüey to Havana for his meeting with Castro was an orchestrated attempt to silence the charismatic Cienfuegos.

The stunning thirty-six-story pre-Castro observation tower and magnificent marble monument of Cuban patriot Jose Martí still anchors the northern end of the *Plaza de la Revolución*—unchanged since the last time I saw it as well.

José Martí was a writer and poet who lost his life on the Dos Rios battlefield during Cuba's War of Independence from

Spain—a ten-year struggle no longer acknowledged as the country's war of independence by today's Cuban government. Cuba's victory over Spain in 1898, they explain, merely led to a new era of "imperialist occupation" by the United States. As a result, they argue, Cuba did not gain its true sovereignty and independence until Castro's rise to power in 1959. I thought about how cynical it was to include José Martí's image on this rebranded plaza if the war of independence he sacrificed his life for is not acknowledged, and the numerous poems and essays on reconciliation, liberty, freedom, and democracy he once wrote are now interpreted to define, defend, and romanticize a political dogma he never represented.

I looked at the José Martí monument again and imagined a teardrop on his cheek.

The Cuban government-controlled tourist buses lined the perimeter of the *Plaza del la Revolución* this morning while scores of foreign tourists took their selfies on the square. Children ran and played, pursuing the invisible friends only they could see, while their mothers chased after them. Everything seemed normal. Little did they understand what they were really seeing.

In this rebranded plaza of paradox and contradictions, Cuba's alternate history is celebrated daily by the government, locals, and tourists alike—but not by George, José, or me today.

All morning, I had experienced intermittent flashes of memories I struggled to understand. They placed me here, in the former *Plaza Civica*, dressed in a Boy Scout uniform during a large gathering. Instinctively, I defended myself from these thoughts by dismissing them as nonsense.

Months later, however, back home with my family in the United States, I mentioned it to my older cousin, Julio.

"Mayito, don't you remember?" Julio asked.

"Remember what?" I replied.

"You and I were Boy Scouts and attended the annual jamboree at the *Plaza Civica*," he said.

He was right; my cousin and I *were* Boy Scouts in Cuba. The last Boy Scout function we attended was the 1959 Jamboree at the former *Plaza Civica*. Shortly thereafter, the Cuban revolutionary government decided that the Boy Scouts organization was a dangerous imperialist import and banned them.

In order to avoid the vitriol and insults from Castro loyalists aimed at anything American or anyone considered to be an American sympathizer, common during those days, my parents warned me never to mention I was a Boy Scout to anyone again. It worked all too well; I did not allow myself to acknowledge my Boy Scout years until Julio reminded me.

"The one constant through all the years has been
baseball ... baseball has marked the time ... it reminds
us of all that once was good, and it could be again."
—Field of Dreams

George, José, and I joined Maidel in his car, waved goodbye to the Che Guevara and Camilo Cienfuegos steel portraits, smiled at the huge Martí monument, and left the *Plaza de la Revolución*. It was time to visit the place where the Cuban baseball gods of my youth once played.

Baseball is a bonding agent among families in Cuba as well as in the United States. Parents take their sons and daughters to ball games. They, in turn, eventually take their own sons and daughters to baseball's cathedrals as well, thus sustaining a tribal ritual continuously repeated throughout generations. Baseball is an ingredient of the chemical composition of many Cuban and American families, including my own. I had the fortune of sharing the love of baseball, first with my father and later with my son. It is an integral part of the family bonds we share.

When I lived in Cuba, my family rooted for the Almendares Scorpions of the Cuban Professional Baseball League and the Cuban Sugar Kings, Havana's AAA International League baseball team. I would ritualistically listen to the play-by-play nightly radio broadcasts of their games or watch them on our family's black-and-white TV set at home. Now and then, my father and I would go see them play at the old Cerro Stadium (the Sugar Kings in the summer and Almendares during the winter months).

Riding in Maidel's official-looking black sedan toward the former Cerro Stadium, now called *Estadio Latinoamericano,* I couldn't help but reminisce about the many baseball games my father and I once watched there. They were always special times for us.

My most vivid memory of a game at the stadium was from the fall of 1959, when the Cuban Sugar Kings played the Minneapolis Millers in a dramatic best-of-seven-games series for the Triple-A International League baseball championship crown.

The teams split the first six games of that most important series, with two going into extra innings and another decided on the final at bat. When an early October snowstorm and frigid weather in Minneapolis shifted the seventh (and deciding) game to Havana, my father wasted no time buying tickets for him and me to attend.

At eight years of age, game 7 could not arrive soon enough for me!

94

The day of game 7 was not the only thing that arrived that championship morning. Unfortunately, I awoke sick that day, having developed a cold with a fever overnight. My mother put me to bed, lathered my chest with Vicks VapoRub, and covered me with heavy wool blankets. She fed me an overdose of orange juice and even made the Cuban cure-all—chicken soup—trying all she could for me to feel better by game time. Nothing she did, however, worked.

My father, I thought, would have to attend the game without me.

Later that afternoon, my father arrived home from work, changed into his game clothes, and walked toward my room to check in on me. My mother stopped him just outside my bedroom door and, using the stern maternal voice I knew so well, warned him, "Don't even think about taking Mayito to the game tonight!"

"Of course, Chinita," my father agreed, uncharacteristically sheepish.

Moments later, he walked into my room and sat on the bed next to me, wanting to talk about the lineups and pitchers announced for the game that night.

Then everything changed. When my mother, oblivious to our baseball conversation, walked into the bathroom and turned on the shower, my father—buoyed by this unexpected opportunity—flashed his we-are-about-to-do-something-really-crazy-grin and winked at me. He touched my forehead, realized my fever had diminished, and asked if I felt well enough to go to the game. Of course, I said yes!

What would you expect?

My father held his index finger in front of his lips, motioned for me to stay quiet, and asked me to dress quickly. I threw on my lucky Sugar Kings clothes, silently followed him out of my

Sevillano home bedroom (shielded by the sound of my mother's shower), and hurriedly climbed down the stairs toward the living room below. With no one around to see us, my father and I ran out the decorative glass and metal-framed front door I once shattered with an errant curveball pretending to be Orlando Peña and soon found ourselves in his blue-and-white 1957 Ford on our way to Cerro Stadium.

Fever or not, we were going to the Triple-A International League Baseball Championship Game!

The gloom and doom that clouded my emotions all day had suddenly changed into the excitement and joy of a most unexpected escape!

We arrived at the stadium, grabbed something to eat, settled into our third base bleacher seats, and watched as nearly three thousand Cuban revolutionary soldiers, armed with pistols and rifles, crowded the field, team dugouts, and baselines before the start of the game. A few minutes later, Fidel Castro entered the stadium and made a triumphant trip around the outfield warning track before reaching his seat—much to the delight of an adoring crowd that greeted him with a standing ovation and rowdy revolutionary chants.

The Triple-A championship baseball game promised to be played that night amid a circus atmosphere of nationalism, political grandstanding, and chest pumping.

My father grew increasingly concerned.

Eventually, the pregame revolutionary antics ended and the game finally began. The lead shifted back and forth throughout the night, leading to a tie game at the start of the bottom half of the ninth inning.

With an opportunity to win the Triple-A championship game at home on their final at bat, the Sugar Kings wasted no time placing runners on first and second base. With most fans in the stadium already on their feet and cheering loudly, Daniel Morejon lined a single to center field, sending the lead runner past third base and barreling toward home plate with the winning run. The umpire watched the catcher's late tag and signaled the runner safe. The Cuban Sugar Kings were the 1959 champions of the Triple-A International Baseball League!

The crowd and my father started to cheer even louder; I screamed as loud as I could too.

(Circa 1959) My father and me watching the Cuban Sugar Kings play during the Triple-A Baseball Championship Game at Cerro Stadium

Then, the celebration grew out of control. Amid all the planned celebratory fireworks, the soldiers began to discharge their weapons into the air. It did not take long before all those *championship* bullets fired toward the nighttime sky started to rain back down onto the bleachers around us.

Extreme happiness had suddenly turned into excruciating fear. My father asked me to lie on the concrete floor between the rows of bleacher seats and positioned his body on top of mine, desperately trying to protect me from harm.

Terrified by the sound of the bullets landing on the seats in front and behind us, we remained motionless on the concrete floor until it was over.

The extracurricular behavior by Castro's revolutionary militia and the dangers it posed to the fans and players in attendance that night did not play well with the commissioner of Major League Baseball. Soon after the game ended, the Cuban Sugar Kings's affiliation with Major League Baseball was rescinded. Unknowingly, I had done more than watch the Cuban Sugar Kings win the Triple-A Baseball Championship Crown that night; I had also witnessed the beginning of the end of Cuban professional baseball.

By midseason in 1960, the Sugar Kings franchise no longer played in Cuba.

Months later, the Cuban Professional Baseball League also came to an end, and with it, my beloved Almendares team as well.

There were plenty of fireworks at the stadium after the Cuban Sugar Kings won the Triple-A championship game that unforgettable night, but not as much as when my father and I arrived back at our Sevillano home in the wee hours of the morning. We knew the time of reckoning with my mother waited for us inside the front door.

With no sound from my mother's shower to mask our entrance back home at that time of night, we could only hope she was asleep.

We laughed and lightheartedly kept raising our index fingers in front of our mouths, reminding ourselves to be as quiet as possible while my father bravely opened our decorative glass and steel-framed front door. Once the door swung open, we were met by the sobering sight of my mother, wide-awake and seated on her rocking chair directly in front of us. She was rocking herself rather aggressively and did not look amused. We were busted!

"Ignacio," implored my mother, "how could you do this?"

My father leaned toward me and nervously whispered in my ear, "Mayito, leave this to me. Go upstairs to bed!"

The last thing I remember hearing my mother say while I ran up our Sevillano marble stairs toward the safety of my second-floor bedroom that night was, "Ignacio, if your son catches pneumonia, it will be your fault!"

I had never been so happy to be sent to bed. My mother was furious with my father, and I wanted no part of her wrath. My grandfather, the family's patriarch and peacekeeper, was nowhere to be found either; he knew better than to get involved in this one as well. My father was on his own, facing an argument he could not possibly win.

Apologetic and contrite, he took one for the team that night—I will always love him for that.

Still Safe at Home Plate

Maidel, José, George, and I arrived at the *Estadio Latinoamericano* this morning, found a parking spot, climbed out of the car, and proceeded to walk toward the ballpark.

Fifty-seven years after the Sugar Kings played that memorable championship game, I was back where it all happened, wearing my vintage Almendares cap, and seeking to bond with the memories of the exciting times my father and I once spent here.

The former Cerro Stadium looked exactly the way I remembered it this morning, seemingly unchanged since the last time I was here. It had recently been repainted with its historical blue color in an effort to freshen its appearance in time for President Obama's visit earlier this year.

Blue was my Almendares team's color. The stadium, I thought, was welcoming me back today.

(May, 2016) Wearing the Almendares baseball cap during my return to the former Cerro Baseball Stadium

I walked to the ticket office, hoping to buy tickets for a ballgame here while I was still in Havana this week. The ticket sales representative, however, informed me that the Cuban League amateur baseball season had recently ended and there were no games scheduled for several weeks.

Since there was no game today, I initially talked myself into just being satisfied with walking around the exterior of the stadium. My expectations soon changed, however, when I noticed an open gate leading directly onto the ballpark's outfield warning track.

Sensing an unplanned opportunity to enter the stadium that once brought me so much joy, I quickly walked through the open gate, and hoped no one was watching.

It did not take long, however, before a burly-but-affable security guard noticed me walking onto the outfield warning track and yelled out, "Brother, where do you think you are going?"

The affable guard quickly caught up with me just inside the outfield's open gate, flashed his best you-should-know-better-than-that look, and smiled. Soon, we were talking like old friends about the stadium's rich history and colorful past.

I showed him my vintage Almendares cap and shared some of my stories about the Almendares and Cuban Sugar Kings baseball games my father and I once watched here. When I told him the story of how my father snuck me out of our home one night—even though I was sick with a mild fever—so we could watch the decisive game 7 of the 1959 Triple-A International League Baseball Championship Series in this stadium, the affable security guard laughed heartily, removed his cap, looked toward the heavens, and declared, "I salute your father for his bravery!"

Once we both stopped laughing, my new baseball friend grew unexpectedly serious and quietly asked, "What do you want to do inside the stadium?"

"I want to sit on the bleachers and remember my times here with my father," I responded. "I will not be here long."

The affable guard looked around us to see who was listening to our conversation and, loud enough for everyone to hear, announced in an official tone of voice, "You can visit the bleachers and reminisce all you want, but you are not allowed to take photographs of the field. Brother, you cannot take your camera inside the stadium."

I turned to my friend George, still standing just outside the outfield warning track's gate, and asked him to take my camera to Maidel's car.

"Please forgive my friend Mario," George told the security guard. "He loves baseball a little too much!"

"That's why I decided to let him in," the affable security guard responded with a genuine smile.

George, who was not as big a baseball fan as me, stepped onto the field, grabbed my camera, and walked out the still-open gate with the affable security guard in tow.

As soon as they left, I climbed the steps leading to the third base grandstands and wandered around the stadium bleachers until I found a seat that reminded me of the general area where my father and I would often sit whenever we watched baseball games here.

I sat on one of the freshly painted blue seats and, for the first time in decades, stared out onto the old Cerro Stadium baseball field once more.

It did not take long for warm memories of my times here with my father to return. I imagined the Almendares and Cuban Sugar King baseball players trotting out of their assigned dugouts to take their positions on the field below me, just before the home plate umpire signaled for the game to begin. Soon, the baseball heroes of my youth were playing on this field of Triple-A champions once more.

I could sense my father's presence sitting beside me with his arm around my shoulders, like he always did, simultaneously watching the game and discussing baseball strategy throughout the night. My heart swelled with love. For a moment, my father and I were together again, enjoying another ball game at Cerro Stadium.

Nothing in the world could have been better this morning.

I looked around and noticed there was no one else in the stadium with me. In a place with fifty-five thousand seats, I was alone—no visitors, no workers, and most importantly, no affable security guard. Since I could not see the guard, I figured he also could not see me.

Emboldened by my newly perceived privacy, I retrieved my cell phone from the front left pocket of my pants and proceeded to take enough photographs and videos to thoroughly document my joyful return to the stadium that once brought me so much joy.

The last time I was here turned out to be one of the most exciting and emotional days of my life. Today, I remembered the warmth of my relationship with the game, the baseball cathedral of my youth, my childhood baseball heroes, and the love of sharing it all with my father.

It was a beautiful morning of baseball memories and father-son bonds.

A few minutes later, it was time to leave. I started my descent down the bleachers and walked toward the same gate I had entered the field from earlier this morning. There, sitting next to the still-open gate, was the affable guard, patiently waiting for me.

"Brother, how are you?" he asked. "Did you enjoy reminiscing inside the ballpark?"

"Yes," I responded, "thank you for allowing me to remember."

The security guard laughed and very quietly, so as not to draw attention or be overheard by anyone eavesdropping, said, "Brother, you had a smile the entire time you were sitting on the bleachers. I sincerely hope you enjoyed recalling your visits here with your father and that the photos and videos you took with your cell phone camera turn out good for you."

"Baseball," I said, doing my best *Field of Dreams* impersonation, "'reminds us of all that once was good and it could be again.'"

He smiled, shook my hand, and whispered, "Someday, my brother, someday."

The affable guard and I had a beautiful bonding experience today. He allowed me to enter the closed stadium this morning by voicing the rules of his decision loud enough for his supervisors to hear. It was what he felt was safest for him to do. Later, in an act of Cuban brotherhood, he looked the other way while I photographed and took videos of the stadium, allowing me to remember and record an important chapter of my childhood here.

Such is the sometimes sweet and often complicated relationship between Cubans on both sides of the Florida Straits.

"Thank you, brother," I said with a smile and discretely handed him a twenty-dollar bill.

"My wife and daughter will appreciate this," the guard said ... and hugged me.

I hugged him back.

Gambling Playground

My friends and I climbed inside Maidel's black Chinese sedan with the dark-tinted windows and settled into our usual seats. We waved goodbye to the affable guard and started our drive toward the Havana Riviera Hotel—an architectural gem once owned by American gangster Meyer Lansky.

The Riviera's modernist facade dominated the Havana skyline across from the Malecon waterfront seawall this morning—its commanding presence and timeless beauty still expressing an elegance and sophistication synonymous with other five-star modernist hotels around the world.

We arrived at the Riviera, climbed out of Maidel's car, and walked past the exquisite exterior fountain and sculptures on our way toward the hotel's entrance.

Once inside, my friends and I proceeded to explore the Riviera with the help of those vintage photographs I had brought inside my three-ring notebook to use as a historical reference during my visit to Cuba.

Comparing those pictures from long ago with the hotel this morning, it was clear to see not much had changed here since the day it opened in 1957. The hotel's magnificent lobby, iconic casino annex (now used as a convention and event space), and the famous Copa Room—whose inaugural show featured Ginger Rogers and once hosted shows by American performers Abbott and Costello, Steve Allen, Mamie Van Doren, William Holden, Ava

Gardner, and Nat King Cole—were still stunningly beautiful and meticulously maintained. Even the art deco-designed pool area and imposing ten-meter diving platform remained as glamorous today as the day they were built.

It was good to see that the Riviera Hotel still stood today as a true gem of Havana's proud architectural past.

Its glory days never seemed to have ended.

The American Embassy

We left the Riviera Hotel and sat in Maidel's car, unsure of where to go next. My friends wanted to go to Hemingway's Floridita bar and spend the rest of the morning enjoying Cuban rum drinks and salsa music. I decided, instead, to walk along Havana's famed waterfront, watch the azure Caribbean waves crash against the Malecon seawall, and rediscover the city's many iconic buildings, sculptures, historical markers, and parks.

I asked Maidel to drop me off at the nearby American Embassy to start my walk before he drove my friends to their watering hole. Minutes later, we arrived at the embassy—I was on my own.

I looked at the American Embassy and contemplated its notable significance. I thought about the countless Cubans who come here seeking passage to freedom, humanitarian assistance, and family reunifications. It made me smile. I also thought about the thousands of others who come here instead to express their profound hatred and vitriol toward the United States—a country they believe to be their archenemy. It saddened me. The conflict between the rage of hate and the forces of good have battled here over the years to no conclusive end.

I longed for the day when the better angels inside us all would finally prevail.

The American electronic ticker tape that for years denounced the Cuban government from atop the American Embassy and the curtain of black flags installed by the Cubans attempting to block all views of the building and its messages are gone now. The hateful demonstrations have stopped, and the American Embassy was officially reopened a few months before I arrived in Cuba this week.

The hope for a new start in Cuban-American relations filled the air around me today.

The sight of the embassy's American flag waving peacefully over Cuban soil filled me with the hope that one day soon the people of the US and Cuba would once again enjoy a relationship built on friendship and trust. I applauded President Obama's message of reconciliation from inside Cuba's *Gran Teatro de la Habana* and imagined a future based on respect and goodwill between our nations.

I wished for the day when the Cuban Diaspora would finally end, allowing Cubans everywhere to walk on Cuban soil as brothers and sisters once more.

The Forest of Flags

I walked toward the nearby Forest of Flags and stared at the American Embassy across the street, still partially obscured by all those tall metallic flagpoles silently waiting for the day when they would once again hoist the curtain of black flags blocking the view of the only building on Cuban soil symbolic of friendship and cooperation between the land of my birth and my country of citizenship.

I ached at the thought of a return to the hatred and vitriol of the past.

(May, 2016) The Cuban Forest of Flags and the American Embassy beyond

The Anti-Imperialist Tribune

Across from the sobering Forest of Flags, a stone's throw away from the American Embassy, is the ominously named Anti-Imperialist Tribune. This public event venue was hastily built in 2000 by the Cuban government as a stage for daily demonstrations against the United States during the Elián González saga.

Elian was a five-year-old boy who unwittingly found himself at the center of a protracted international political crisis between the United States and Cuba. He had barely survived a fateful ocean crossing from Cuba to the United States when, on Thanksgiving Day 1999, an American fisherman miraculously found him alone and clinging to the inside of an inner tube aimlessly floating on the high seas.

By then, his mother and most of the other passengers aboard the doomed small boat trying to reach Miami had already drowned. Elian moved in with his extended family in Miami. On the opposite side of the Florida Straits, Castro wanted him back with his father in Cuba.

The political and human drama about the future of a five-year-old boy played daily amid heightened human emotions and political rhetoric. The constant drum of virulent and hateful demonstrations in Havana's Anti-Imperialist Tribune and on the streets of Miami's Little Havana tugged at the hearts and souls of the world as it watched this sordid spectacle play on for months. Eventually, Elian was forcibly removed from his family's home in the United States and returned to Cuba.

Many Cubans in Havana rejoiced. Most Cubans in Miami, like me, wept.

Cuba's Veiled Oppression

Searching for a higher vantage point from which to take panoramic photos and videos of the scenic Havana district surrounding the Anti-Imperialist Tribune, I decided to climb up the red ramp leading to its stage. Halfway up the ramp, however, I was startled by a loud and aggressive whistle emanating from three young men walking toward me with the unequivocal cadence of trouble.

Once they arrived at the base of the ramp, one of them motioned aggressively for me to join them. Instinctively, I knew I had to diffuse the situation.

"Young men, how can I help you?" I solicited in a premeditated fatherly tone.

"Old man, I am the one who may decide to help you," responded one of the three comrades whose physique reminded me of *Popeye*.

"What is going on here?" I asked.

By now, however, I knew exactly who these people were. In Cuba, the first layer of security falls on plain clothed security agents whose job is to blend in with the population and confront anyone who seems suspicious or is disturbing the peace. A disagreeable response or anti-revolutionary expression could result in being thrown into a van with dark-tinted windows for further interrogation.

"Why are you walking up the red ramp to the Tribune stage?" *Popeye* wanted to know.

"I want to film a panoramic video from the stage's higher vantage point showing the American Embassy, Malecon Waterfront, Tribune Park, Morro Fortress, and the modernist Vedado district buildings beyond," I responded.

A second, somewhat older and calmer, plain clothed agent smiled and responded, "You know, he's right. The view is better from up there."

Popeye did not smile. Neither did the third young man, a slim, tall, and passive-aggressive agent who, after quietly staring at me throughout our conversation, finally asked, "You are not from around here, are you?"

"No, I'm from South Florida," I said.

"Oh," he sighed, as hot air seemed to leave his body, "you are from the Community."

Cubans on the island today refer to Cubans living abroad as being from "the Community." Being a tourist from "the Community" probably saved me from a very unpleasant afternoon. The Cuban government's oppression of their own citizens does not apply to tourists, especially Americans or Cuban-Americans.

After an awkward moment of silence, *Popeye* walked to within inches of my face, gave me his most intimidating look, and sharing his bad breath with my nostrils, said, "If you promise not to climb the red ramp, old man, I will let you go."

"All right, I won't. Just stop calling me an old man," I said, feigning hurt feelings.

Popeye and his comrades gave me a repugnant look, shook their heads in disgust, and walked away. I was happy to see them leave; I had not come to Cuba to be interrogated by undercover security agents. I aborted my climb up the red ramp to the Anti-Imperialistic Tribune stage and abandoned my plans for the Oscar-worthy artistic panorama video I was planning to film from up there. Photos and videos from the Malecon boardwalk would have to suffice today.

I resumed walking along the Malecon Waterfront under the cover of a blue Caribbean sky, warmed by the hot Cuban sun, caressed by the constant Malecon Waterfront breeze, and serenaded by the relentless sounds of waves crashing upon the seawall below me. Soon, my unpleasant experience at the Anti-Imperialist Tribune became just a distant memory—I could not imagine being anywhere else on earth.

The Missing American Eagle

A few minutes later, I arrived at the imposing and historical Maine Monument. In 1898, the American battleship USS *Maine* was blown up while docked in Havana's harbor, resulting in the tragic death of 260 American servicemen. As a result of the blast, the American government declared war on Spain and sent military troops into Cuba to fight alongside Cuban freedom fighters. Together, they ended the long and bloody Cuban struggle against the Spanish occupation of the island, assuring Cuba's independence from Spain.

American history blames the explosion as an act of war by the Spanish colonial forces. Cuban revisionist history today, however, explains how the United States destroyed its own battleship and sacrificed the lives of their own soldiers in an attempt to blame Spain for the blast and create an excuse to invade and take over the island of Cuba.

The iconic American eagle that once crowned the Maine Monument was removed during the early days of the Cuban Revolution. Fortunately, the remaining monument, with its sculptures and engravings, was allowed to remain.

The original Maine Monument's inscription quoting an 1898 US Congressional resolution on the future of Cuba still faces inward toward central Havana and humbly states, "*The people of Cuba have the right to live free and independent.*" In 1960, however, Castro's revolutionary government added an additional plaque to the monument, defiantly looking north over the Florida Straits toward the United States. This one, however, reads, "*To the victims of the Maine who were sacrificed as a result of the Imperialists' voracity and desire to take over the island of Cuba.*"

I took a deep breath and sighed. Cuban revolutionary dubious truths, historical revisionism, and hateful rhetoric are sometimes difficult to swallow.

José and George arrived in Maidel's black Chinese sedan with the dark-tinted windows and motioned for me to join them. They peppered me with stories about their visit to Hemingway's Floridita bar and then listened incredulously to the story of my meeting with *Popeye* and his comrades. Maidel informed us that these confrontations are a constant irritant of Cuba's reality today. Once the agents realized I was a tourist, he said, they had to let me go. We took a collective breath and decided to go visit the nearby University of Havana.

The Promised Steps Never Taken

When I was a young boy, my father would often drive past the University of Havana, point to the monumental steps leading to the school's entrance portal, and tell me, "Mayito, someday you will climb those steps and attend college here."

I would often imagine how proud my family would feel the first time I'd walk through the marble portal at the top of those steps and onto the university grounds, signaling my transition from a schoolboy into a college student. Unfortunately, it was never meant to be. Instead, I attended the University of Florida, where I excelled in my studies and graduated magna cum laude from its School of Architecture, realizing my Cuban childhood dream of becoming an architect.

I owe the refinement of my talents, intellectuality, and professional career to my education at the University of Florida. I am, and will always be, a Florida Gator. Still, in my original universe, I would have been thrilled to have attended my predestined school.

Today, I would not be climbing those steps for the first time alone—George and José were coming with me.

During the time it took Maidel to drive the short distance from the Maine Monument to the University of Havana, I grew increasingly excited at the thought that today—fifty-six years after leaving Cuba—I would finally walk up the steps my father assured me I would one day climb and enter the university I once dreamed of attending.

On May 18, 2016, I proudly walked up the University of Havana's monumental marble steps, deliberately and slowly completing each step never taken. By the time I entered the campus through the school's marbled entry gateway with *"Universidad de la Habana"* carved into its facade, I realized I had finally taken my promised steps.

I just never imagined it would have taken so long.

A man named Lazaro approached us as soon as my friends and I reached the top of the university's monumental entrance. He identified himself as a calculus professor and volunteered to take us on a guided tour of the school. Seconds later, we were walking through campus with him.

It did not take long, however, before my friends and I realized that touring the University of Havana with Lazaro was a mistake. We expected academic descriptions of the campus buildings and tales of accomplishments from its many notable graduates. What we got instead was a well-rehearsed series of exaggerated pro-revolutionary narratives singularly focused on the many anti-imperialist declarations, revolutionary sacrifices, and pro-Castro speeches made from different vantage points throughout the university.

Eventually, Lazaro went too far. When he claimed that prior to Castro's revolution black students paid twice the tuition as everyone else, José (who, like Lazaro, is a black Cuban man) walked away from us toward the university's Plaza Cardenas to call his mother in Miami.

A few minutes later, once we caught up with him, a visibly agitated José stared down Lazaro with a defiant glare and said, "Lazaro, I just spoke with my black mother who attended the University of Havana during the 1940s. She told me that during her time here as a student, everyone paid the same tuition. What you said earlier is not true. I am done with your revolutionary speeches and propaganda. I am out of here!"

George put his arm around José and escorted him away from Lazaro. The tour was over for them. I, however, chose not to leave. I had waited too long to be here. I asked Lazaro to tone down his exaggerated political rhetoric and continued my tour with him.

I'm glad I did. For the next hour or so, I immersed myself in the excitement of walking through my predestined school for the first time, feeling much like a freshman student during college orientation weekend. Young men and women walked out of the classroom buildings around me with their books tucked inside the backpacks they carried slung over their shoulders. Some sat in the courtyards lost in conversation or doing homework. Others walked around, acting busy on their cell phones. Now and then, someone would acknowledge me with a simple hello.

Lost in the sights and sounds of my once-promised school, I realized that any of them could have, would have, been me.

I thought about how, in my alternate Cuban life, I would have called home by now to report on my first day of school at the University of Havana. It would have been a wonderful accomplishment, worthy of celebrating with my extended family.

I wondered how different my life would have been if not for Castro's rise to power.

When my tour came to an end, I thanked Lazaro and reached to retrieve my wallet from the front right pocket of my pants. "Don't give me a tip here, please. Let's go somewhere more private," Lazaro said and led me to a corner of the campus surrounded by massive columns, partial walls, solid railings, and tall landscaping.

Once there, the well-rehearsed professor sighed, stared down at his feet, and meekly mentioned, "Brother, please give me a good tip. The salary I get paid here is so meager that I can hardly afford to eat."

Lazaro's revolutionary fervor and exaggerated narrative was finished. His well-rehearsed farce had reached its end. The charade was over. The reality of the Cuban Revolution's failure and the sad truth of his daily life were now in the open. His reliance on a tip from a Cuban-American who once fled the very same revolution he still defended said it all. There was no need for additional words now. We both understood our alternate realities.

I gave him a twenty-dollar bill, almost the equivalent of a month's paycheck in Cuba—he gave me a thankful and sad smile.

I felt bad for Lazaro; he was just trying to survive the day.

El Parque Central District

My friends and I left the University of Havana and headed toward the iconic *Parque Central* (Central Park) District, with its magnificent architecture, iconic statue of José Martí, and spicy *Esquina Caliente* (Hot Corner), where scores of sports fans gather daily to discuss any topic with all the enthusiasm, passion, and exuberance Cubans can summon.

Once there, we watched as several even-tempered fans talked about the historical relevance of soccer great Lionel Messi, debating whether he was the best soccer player in history. I was disappointed; Cuba, I thought, was synonymous with baseball—not soccer. I had expected to hear a spirited baseball argument, not a civilized soccer debate.

I stood on the *Esquina Caliente* still wearing my Almendares baseball cap and waited for someone to recognize it. No one, however, seemed to notice. Finally, a young man looked at the big blue letter *A* on my white cap and shouted out, "Oakland Athletics, right?"

"No," I said, "the A's colors are green and yellow."

He looked at me with a dumbfounded look on his face and asked, "Well, then, what team is it?"

"Almendares," I said.

"Never heard of them," he responded.

No one in the *Esquina Caliente* seemed to know much about pre-Castro Cuban baseball that day. It saddened me.

Happy Days, Frankensteins, and Much More

The *Parque Central* District is the heart of Havana's tourist sector. Even though you see government- and privately owned vintage 1950s American automobiles, trucks, and motorcycles all over Cuba—here is where the most colorful and meticulously refurbished *Happy Days* cars are lined up and available for hire as taxies.

It is a dazzling sight. Their bright exterior colors, gleaming interior finishes, and shiny chrome transform these magnificent vehicles into irresistible magnets for the curious visitors.

The always-creative Cuban entrepreneurial spirit is alive and well here too. Well-dressed car owners stand next to their shiny vintage cars and are quick to enter into a conversation with anyone pausing to admire them. Eventually, they will offer you a taxi ride through Havana.

While the tourists drool over these beautiful vehicles, reminiscent of a time long ago, local Cubans lovingly refer to them as "Frankensteins." An exquisitely painted candy-red-and-white 1957 Chevy might have a transmission from a 1979 Russian Lada and a radiator adapted to fit from a Fiat. The chrome trims might be, in fact, aluminum recently shaped at a local shop.

It all works perfectly. The sight of these delicious vintage vehicles cruising through a city still defined by the sights and sounds synonymous with the simpler days associated with the lifestyle of the 1950s provides for the imagery and romance of a place and time many long for and find only in Cuba.

The *Parque Central* is Havana's magical district.

Sometimes, however, the Cuban entrepreneurial spirit can get a little too creative.

"Can I interest you in a ride through Havana?" offered the owner of a shiny blue-and-white 1957 Ford Fairlane, similar to the one my father once owned.

"No," José said, "we already have a driver."

"Are you guys then looking for a hot *mulata*?" responded the well-dressed entrepreneur.

"No, thanks," José, George, and I responded in unison.

"Okay, no hot Cuban woman for you boys from Miami," the Fairlane owner summed up. "How about cigars? I have a friend who works in the factory. Place your order now and I can have a box of freshly rolled Cohibas ready for you to pick up later tonight. I'll only charge you half of what you would have paid on the factory tour, and the box will have the official seal. It won't be a problem getting it through customs at the airport."

George, José, and I just shook our heads and smiled.

"Cuba," I told my friends, "sure has a complicated economy."

(May, 2016) Vintage cars near El Parque Central

The *Parque Central* District also includes several beautiful and historical buildings, synonymous with Cuba's great architectural past, including the *Gran Teatro de la Habana* (Great Theater of Havana) and the Cuban Capitol building. Together they form the most recognizable and iconic images of the central Havana skyline.

The *Gran Teatro de la Habana*, formerly known as the *Centro Gallego* (Galician Center), was built in 1914. It is famous for its striking neobaroque architecture, acclaimed for its world-class theater, and renowned for hosting performances from scores of celebrated Cuban and international artists, including Ernesto Lecuona and Enrico Caruso.

My father, being of Galician descent, would often visit this magnificent center with my mother or his accountant friends. Over the years, he shared many stories about his times here, including descriptions of the center's opulent interiors and sophisticated theater performances.

To me, however, *El Gran Teatro* will always represent President Obama's historical, moving, and inspirational speech delivered flawlessly from its theater's stage on March 21, 2016. On that day, Obama's opening words, *"Cultivo una rosa blanca,"* quoted Cuban patriot José Martí's nineteenth-century poem of reconciliation and offered a twenty-first-century bridge of hope, peace, and unity from Havana to Key West. His speech, watched in stunned silence by Cuba's leaders inside the theater and millions of people on the island and abroad, called on Cuba's youth to forge their own future and challenged Castro's government to allow them to plant the seeds of change.

Obama inspired young Cubans throughout the island that day, serving them a dose of life-changing "oxygen" and a plate full of hope for a future defined by *El Cambio*.

Today, the *Gran Teatro de la Habana* stared back at me with all its magnificent architectural beauty and rich history. I imagined my father's raspy voice and contagious laughter inside its walls and envisioned the echoes of Obama's words still resonating from the theater's stage. I looked intently at the former *Centro Gallego*, felt the warmth of my father's unconditional love, and inhaled Cuba's new "oxygen" of hope into the deepest recesses of my lungs.

Across the street from the *Gran Teatro* is *El Capitolio Cubano* (Cuba's Capitol building), home to the pre-Castro Cuban Congress and a tangible reminder of the country's bicameral democratic past. Soon after the Cuban Revolution of 1959, Fidel Castro dissolved the Cuban Congress and closed the Capitol, keeping the building mostly abandoned and silent all these years. For decades, generations of Cubans walked by the Cuban Capitol's domed facade, ignoring its presence and unaware of its historical significance.

Today, however, change was in the air. The Capitol was in the midst of a multiyear meticulous and historically accurate renovation of its original design, after which it was slated to reclaim its role as the seat of Cuba's government once more. It was good to see this majestic and historical structure finally receiving the attention it had always deserved.

I hoped that the rebirth of this most symbolic Cuban building would serve as a metaphor and inspiration for a country thirsty for the early stages of economic and political reforms.

Lunch on My Parents' Shopping Street

By now it was midafternoon; and José, George, and I were hungry and ready for lunch. Maidel wanted us to experience the difference in food and service between the privately owned *Paladares* restaurants we visited the last couple of days and a typical government-owned restaurant, like *Lluvia de Oro*. We left the Cuban Capitol Building and headed toward the historic *Calle Obispo*, a pedestrian shopping street frequented by my parents during the 1940s and 1950s, on our way to a much-needed lunch.

Calle Obispo dates from the 1600s and is lined with Spanish colonial, art deco, and modernist buildings—including the former La Moderna Poesia bookstore, Havana Wall Street Bank (now the Ministry of Finance), the iconic Florida Hotel, the Ambos Mundos Hotel (where Hemingway often worked and slept)—and an assortment of art galleries, restaurants, shops, and boutiques, including a most interesting bookstore ran by two hippie-looking young Cuban entrepreneurs.

Inside the hippies' store, neat rows of new and used books categorized into José Martí, Russian History, Colonial Cuba, American History, American Baseball, Literature, Hemingway, and Cuban Revolution aisles filled every inch of available space. At the entrance to the shop, and leaning over the obligatory Che Guevara poster, however, was a large lithography of the famous Rolling Stones lips for sale. It made me laugh.

A sign posted on the shop's storefront reading "We Speak English" effectively summed up the essence of the hippies' bookstore. Their business, like Cuba, was a place full of contradictions.

By the time my friends and I arrived at *Lluvia de Oro* restaurant, it was already close to three in the afternoon. No wonder we were starving!

The *Lluvia de Oro* served us much more than good Cuban food this afternoon. It also provided us with an education on the difference between privately owned *Paladares* and government-run restaurants in Havana today. The *Paladares* restaurants we visited the last couple of days provided full menus with a wide variety of entrées and voiced no objections to customizing selections or substituting side dishes. Their service was prompt and courteous. Our experience at the state-run *Lluvia de Oro* Restaurant was, well, different.

Except for a couple of Canadian tourists wasting the afternoon away sipping mojitos at the bar, the *Lluvia de Oro* was essentially empty. Three uniformed waiters leaned against the bar counter lost in a deep conversation among themselves. Too busy to greet my friends and me, they directed us with an emphatic tilt of their heads toward a dining area filled with empty tables decorated only with single paper menus serving as placemats.

We arrived at our table, looked over the five-entrée choices on the menu, and prepared to order lunch. Now and then, the waiters would glance at us and briefly smile before resuming their conversation. Eventually, after what seemed like an eternity, they reached a satisfactory conclusion to their discussion and one of them made his way toward our table with all the speed and determination of a sloth in the hot midday Cuban sun.

The expression-challenged uniformed waiter finally reached our table and stared past us with an aloof and vacant look in his eyes. There was no "Hello" or "Welcome to *Lluvia de Oro* Restaurant" small talk from our waiter today. He just stared out into nowhere and announced to no one in particular, "We have no fish or malta today."

With a menu consisting of only a few selections and minimal fixed side dishes, we were left with a very limited choice of chicken, salad, or chicken soup.

"Please bring me the chicken filet," I said. "Hold the onions and add some wedges of lime."

"No custom orders are allowed," the undemonstrative waiter responded. "The chicken comes with onions. You can remove them yourself if you like. The lime wedges will be an additional charge."

Too hungry to debate our waiter, I ordered the chicken entrée, removed the onions myself, and paid for the wedges of lime. The meal and the music were fine. The Cuban coffee, however, was as disappointing as the service.

Moliendo Café (Grinding Coffee)

One of the Cuban cultural traditions I always thought would never change was Cuban coffee. A cup of this sweet caffeine normally starts or concludes deep and meaningful conversations among family and friends. The traditional Cuban coffee meticulously mixes the coffee with sugar during the brewing process, producing an *espumita* (sugar foam) atop and throughout the drink. Restaurants and families alike have historically taken great pride in creating their own secret brewing process aimed at concocting a sweet coffee worthy of celebrating the conclusion of a Cuban meal.

In most Havana restaurants today, however, Cuban coffee is merely an espresso. There is no secret *espumita* process. Each person just applies the sweetener of their choosing. Today, the exclamation point of Cuban cuisine lives on in Miami but, incredibly, not in Havana.

Even the venerable Cuban coffee has become an immigrant.

"Rhythm Is Gonna Get You"
—*Gloria Estefan and the Miami Sound Machine*

Music seems to surround you everywhere you go in Havana. It is a constant of life here and synonymous with the Cuban culture. The restaurants, shops, and hotels of Obispo Street were alive with music as we left the restaurant this afternoon. José and George decided to go with Maidel to *La Bodeguita del Medio* for more drinks and music. I chose to continue my sightseeing of central Havana. Later tonight we would meet in our hotel lobby for a night out at the world-famous Tropicana Cabaret.

The Harbor

Alone for the second time today, I walked the remaining section of Obispo Street toward the Havana Harbor inlet boardwalk, across from the Morro Fortress. I wanted to enjoy the views of the Morro and bond with the many Cubans who come here daily to celebrate the red hues of the setting sun over the Caribbean Sea. Before I knew it, I was there.

The Morro fortress and its lighthouse, built as a military bastion for the defense of Havana in 1589, have long been a beacon of nautical safety and a symbol of welcome for the numerous ships, returning nationals, and tourists arriving at Havana's harbor. Today, they welcomed me back.

I sat on the concrete inlet seawall and watched as the Morro's old stones slowly changed colors in concert with the setting sun's transforming light. The constant chatter and youthful laughter from the dozens of teenage boys and girls around me, jumping into the bay and fishing off the seawall, added a most perfect touch of humanity to an already beautiful and serene experience.

Not far from me, young couples in love also watched the setting sun, holding each other's hands and stealing youthful kisses at will. I couldn't help but think about how a mere ninety miles away, in Key West, a similar scene was surely taking place under the same setting sun.

Youth, innocence, and love, after all, are not defined by political borders.

(May, 2016) El Morro fortress and lighthouse

If Cars Could Talk

I remembered how when I was four years old, my family booked a trip on the Havana—Key West overnight ferry. That weekend, we started our weeklong vacation to Miami Beach by sailing through the very same harbor and inlet now in front of me. When we arrived in Key West that morning long ago, my father drove our car off the ferry, looked mischievously at me, and said, "Mayito, this car is so smart that it knows we are in the United States. When I turn on the radio, it will know to speak in English and play rock and roll."

I listened in amazement as our car's radio proved him right.

My dad, I remember thinking that day, *is a genius.*

Now older and wiser, I stared at the Havana Harbor inlet again and smiled at the memory of my father's wit. I took a deep breath of nostalgia and resumed my walk along the harbor inlet boardwalk, stopping long enough to admire the magnificent hillside mounted statue of the Christ of Havana. I had forgotten all about this statue. It was good to rediscover an old friend.

My Grandfather's Ride Home

A few minutes later, I arrived at the nearly empty Casablanca Ferry Plaza—a place I remembered with much childhood delight. My father and I would often come here and wait for my grandfather to arrive on the cross-inlet ferry from his job at the Casablanca Railway Station across the harbor before driving him home in our family car.

Back then, the Casablanca Ferry Plaza was usually crowded with hundreds of passengers coming and going. People would stop and buy snacks from the street vendors beneath the seafaring sounds of dozens of seagulls circling above, landing only to eat the scraps of food that fell on the ground. Music played here once, interrupted by the shouts of lottery vendors selling dreams to the dreamers. My father and I would frequently interact with the ferry passengers, vendors, and sightseers who passed through here. With a little luck, I remembered my father often telling me, we might even catch a glimpse of *El Caballero de Paris*—an educated, beloved, and sometimes homeless street character who would gladly share his philosophies of life, religion, or politics with anyone he met.

I was not a fan. He always seemed a little creepy to me.

Today, all that was gone, replaced only by scores of Cubans fishing for food, jumping in the bay, or seeking distraction from their daily struggles.

El Paseo del Prado

My final stroll today took me on the scenic *Paseo del Prado* promenade, a historical Havana landmark providing a direct pedestrian link between the Havana Harbor Inlet and *El Parque Central*.

This beautiful promenade, illuminated by the bucolic colors of the early-evening tropical light, provided a restful recess to what had been another exciting and emotional day in Cuba. Dozens of people joined me on my leisurely stroll this afternoon, while others sat on the white marble benches lining the perimeter of the promenade. Skateboarders whisked past everyone, showcasing their well-rehearsed tricks and impressive athleticism while still finding the time to smile at all those who watched them. Mature trees enriched the whole experience, casting long shadows announcing the fast-approaching end of daylight.

I walked slowly on the *Paseo del Prado* this afternoon, making sure to absorb every beautiful moment around me. It was an experience I did not want to soon forget.

"Almendares!" a man's voice suddenly shouted out.

He was, of course, referring to the cap I had worn for three days in Cuba and only one person before him had recognized.

"Yes, it is!" I shouted back.

I walked toward the sound of the voice and met Oscar, an elderly man sitting on one of the marble benches at the perimeter of the promenade.

"It's good to see the Almendares cap again," Oscar sighed. "I was a big Almendares fan, you know. Looks like you were too."

"Yes," I said, "Almendares was my team. Do you know that you are only the second person in Havana this week to recognize my cap?"

"Oh," he said, "it doesn't surprise me. No one in Cuba knows anything about the Cuban Professional Baseball League anymore. Castro erased them from history."

"Did he also erase the Cuban Sugar Kings?" I asked.

"Yes, them too," Oscar informed me. "Did you know the Sugar Kings won the 1959 Triple-A International League Championship in Havana's Cerro Stadium?"

That started a conversation that shifted back and forth between the Almendares and Cuban Sugar Kings baseball players we remembered, the positions they played on the field, and their place in the batting order.

When I told him the story of how my father smuggled me out of our house even though I was sick so we could attend the Cuban Sugar Kings' Triple-A championship game, Oscar started to laugh and said, "I would have loved to have met your father. He was courageous."

"Yes, he was," I responded. "He was my father and best friend. He really took one for the team that night. After the game ended and we arrived back home, my mother really let him have it!"

"My wife," Oscar added, "was a big Almendares and Sugar Kings fan, like us. Too bad she passed away a couple of years ago. She would have loved meeting you today."

"I would have loved meeting her too," I said.

"For many years," Oscar continued, "my wife and I would sit on this same bench and watch the parade of characters that walked through here while our sons played in the promenade beyond. They were beautiful times, you know, perfect in every way. All that has changed now. My wife is gone, and my sons live in Miami—I am all alone. This is the only place where I can still feel their love, so I come here every day in order to remember."

Oscar and I had bonded in the most beautiful of ways. He reminded me of my father, and I reminded him of his sons. We transported ourselves to a time and place of baseball teams and heroes lost to the indifference of time, politics, and the Cuban Diaspora. We were alike in so many ways that it was easy for us to become instant friends.

A few minutes later, with night quickly descending upon us, I stood up from the marble bench Oscar and I were sharing and prepared to leave. He looked up with sadness in his eyes and asked me to help him stand up.

Once he was on his feet, my new baseball friend vigorously shook my hand, hugged me, and said, "I haven't spoken about the Sugar Kings or Almendares baseball teams with anyone for over thirty years. Thank you for this beautiful afternoon. You have no idea how much I needed this."

"Me too," I said. "Me too."

I hugged him back and said goodbye.

I felt strangely fulfilled. I am sure he did as well. We both had the connection we had started the day looking for.

It was sad leaving Oscar behind—he was all alone again.

Rum, Oxygen, and Hope

I walked to the end of the *Paseo del Prado* and took a taxi back to the hotel. It was getting late; and I still had to shower, get dressed, and meet my friends for a night out at the world-famous Tropicana Cabaret.

A little over an hour later, freshly showered, energized, and anxious to spend an evening of Cuban fun and music, I joined my friends and climbed into Maidel's black Chinese sedan with the dark-tinted windows. Soon, we were on our way to the Tropicana.

After such an emotional day, I was ready to let loose.

Over the years, I had heard many stories about this beautiful open-air theater, famous for its atmosphere and opulent shows. Opened in 1939, the Tropicana Cabaret consists of a large semicircular guest area with continuous rows of tables neatly lined up end-to-end where visitors sit to watch the show, eat, and drink. The main stage leads to multiple levels of concentric mezzanines surrounding the guests, enabling the show's cast to sing and dance all around the viewing audience. With pulsating performances emanating from seemingly everywhere in the theater at once, it is impossible not to sing, dance, or tap your feet.

George, José, and I sang and moved with the music and dancers all night.

The show tonight was over two and a half-hour long and included well over a hundred singers and dancers. It was an amazing spectacle, unlike anything my friends and I had ever seen. All night long, George, José, and I snacked on appetizers, smoked Cohiba cigars, and drank our share of Havana Club rum—enough that when, at the conclusion of the show, one of the Tropicana dancers asked me to dance with her on stage, to my surprise, I accepted. Looking at the video George took of my dancing, I did not do too badly!

Rum and Cuban music will do that to you.

José, however, drank way too much Havana Club rum. Right before the start of the grand finale, he went for a walk and had not returned.

After my "dancing exhibition" with the Tropicana dancer ended, George and I grew concerned with our friend's whereabouts and decided to go look for him. A few nervous minutes later, we finally found him inexplicably wandering on the street in front of the cabaret's entrance, holding his Tropicana glass still half full of Havana Club rum.

"José, what are you doing in the middle of the road?" I yelled at him.

He gave me a dazed look, took two steps backward followed by one step forward, composed himself briefly, looked at me cross-eyed, and said, "Man, where are the bathrooms in this place?"

Classic!

Too much rum and Cuban music will do that to you too!

Leaving the Tropicana Cabaret, José wanted to continue celebrating the night. Maidel knew exactly where to go and proceeded to drive us to a privately owned club inside a renovated two-story home in a residential district of Havana.

The line of young Cuban nationals waiting to go inside the club that night was impressive. Fortunately, Maidel, being friends with the club's owner, had already arranged for us to skip the line and go directly inside.

José, still drinking from his Tropicana glass, did his best to walk a straight line toward the club's entry doors.

Everything was going perfectly as planned until ...

"*Oye*, you cannot bring that Tropicana glass in here," the no-nonsense bouncer at the club's entrance growled.

"What glass?" José demanded to know.

George took the half-full Tropicana glass out of José's hands, emptied it, and returned it to Maidel's car. Crisis averted, José, George, and I safely walked inside the club.

The place was filled with a young and festive Cuban clientele that night. There were no foreign tourists in sight. Most everyone danced and sang to the music of salsa and reggaeton videos playing on a two-story-high screen mounted on a wall next to the dancing area. Others lined up, three persons deep, to order drinks from a well-stocked bar. On the mezzanine level above the bar, couples shared moments and enjoyed their time together sitting at tables with a great view of the crowded dance floor below.

Everyone was having fun.

As the late evening turned into the predawn hours, the club's DJ became unexpectedly bolder. It was well after two in the morning when the music and videos of banned Cuban-American artists—including Gloria Estefan, Chirino, and Pitbull—began to play, a daring and brazen affront to Cuban revolutionary law.

No one, except me, seemed concerned. The waitresses continued cruising the club and catering to the patrons. Everyone just kept drinking and dancing.

I just ordered another glass of Havana Club and smiled.

All night I was surprised by the seven-dollar-per-drink charge at the club, representing approximately a fourth of the typical Cuban monthly income. Wondering how any Cuban national could afford to buy a drink here, I started asking them.

Most of the club's patrons I spoke with during the night told me they had recently started small businesses, including bed-and-breakfast inns, *Paladares* restaurants, taxi services, and IT assistance companies. Others owned plumbing, auto repair, and electronic shops. Some bragged about their incomes and how they had even purchased homes with their profits.

They were all here simply celebrating their new entrepreneurial spirit and improving fortunes.

Maidel, it turned out, was one of them as well. No wonder he brought us here!

These intrepid young Cuban men and women were busy creating a new generation of Cuban dreamers and neocapitalists with expectations of improving their lives by taking advantage of new laws and opportunities recently enacted by the Cuban government. Their youthful optimism and dreams of a better future were palpable everywhere inside the club. I found myself drinking and dreaming with them throughout the remainder of the night.

In the early hours of the morning, having lost all my inhibitions, I decided to visit a young man and woman I had noticed drinking glass after glass of Cuban rum while hosting several groups of people at their table.

"Good evening," I said. "I've noticed that many of the patrons in the club tonight have visited with you. Everyone here seems to know you. Do you own this place?"

"No, I don't own this club," the young man responded, "but I'm glad you came to visit with me. Many of my friends have been asking me about you too. They want to know why you care so much about their financial ability to buy drinks here. Who are you?"

"I'm a Cuban-American visiting Havana for the first time since I left many years ago," I responded. "I just want to learn all I can about Cuba's reality today."

Seemingly satisfied by my answer, the young man smiled and said, "Good, I thought you were with the government. My name is Pedro, and I am an accountant. I started my private accounting firm last year."

"Well then," I asked, "what are you doing drinking in a bar at three in the morning on a weekday? Don't you need to be in your office in a few hours?"

He looked at me curiously, laughed, and said, "I come here a couple of times a week and look for people I don't recognize, like you. If they have the disposable income to buy seven-dollar drinks, odds are they are new entrepreneurs like me. I befriend them and offer my company's services. Most of the people here tonight are my clients. That's why they all come to talk with me sooner or later."

Pedro had a true entrepreneurial spirit. Astonishingly, he was in the club networking for new clients at three in the morning ... on a weekday no less!

I looked at him, smiled, and continued our conversation. There were still many things I wanted to know.

"Why did you decide to become a private business entrepreneur at this time?" I prodded.

"I don't want to be like my grandfather," he said. "He has lived in so much misery and suffered for so long that he just wants to die."

"I'm sorry," I sighed.

"I don't want to be like my father either," the young accountant continued. "He feels betrayed by the revolution, does not trust anyone, and has given up."

"So then what do you want?" I asked.

"Look around us," he said. "What we *all* want is to be our own generation and change the horrible reality in which Cubans have lived for too long."

"Can you do this?" I said.

"Yes, we have oxygen now," he responded using the slogan we first heard at the *Paladar San Cristobal* yesterday. "We all dream of *El Cambio*."

I shook his hand, smiled proudly at him, and exclaimed, "Never stop breathing that oxygen of hope. Go forge your own future. Become the sole author of your success story."

Young Cubans all over the island are creating a new generation of private business entrepreneurs seeking to improve their quality of life. Individually, they are starting businesses and buying real estate. Together, they are building a nascent middle class not seen here since 1959. These young Cubans are not going anywhere; they are too busy putting down roots. They dream of a future in Cuba, not the United States.

I said goodbye to Pedro, caught up with José and George at their selected stools—tucked in a corner of the club's well-stocked first-floor bar—and surrendered once more to the night's rum and fun. Before we knew it, however, the time of night arrived when it was simultaneously too late to go to sleep and too early to wake up. In a moment of sobriety, we decided to call it a night.

We left the club around four in the morning, climbed into Maidel's car, and started our drive back to the Hotel Nacional.

Another Improbable and Emotional Day

A few minutes later, safely back inside my hotel room, I tucked myself in bed and tried to place my thoughts and emotions into context. Today, I had returned to the rebranded *Plaza Civica*, discovered the cultural heritage and patrimony inherited by my birthright, visited with the baseball gods of my youth, felt the love and special bond I once enjoyed with my father, and met another Almendares and Cuban Sugar Kings baseball fan. I proudly climbed the monumental steps leading to my predestined university, visited Havana Harbor, and returned to the Casablanca Ferry Plaza without having to greet the creepy Caballero de Paris. I experienced a glimpse of the systematic oppression that constantly clouds Cuban life and felt the hope born from President Obama's inspiring words inside *El Gran Teatro de la Habana*. Tonight, I enjoyed the sights and sounds of the Tropicana Cabaret with my friends and met the young men and women busy crafting a generational transition in Cuba. I allowed myself to drink and dream with the dreamers, inhale their oxygen of hope, and celebrate the bright and colorful light born out of the prism of a new beginning.

It had been another improbable, surprising, and emotional day in Cuba.

I tried to fall asleep, but at first, I could not. Cuba was changing; I was changing. I needed time to process it all. Still wide-awake at almost five in the morning, I decided that my deepest thoughts would have to wait for another day. I took a deep breath and told myself everything was going to be okay.

Finally, alone with my thoughts and lost within the swirls of my consciousness, I found my peace, eased my mind, and slowly drifted into a blissful sleep.

(May, 2016) The Tropicana Cabaret

DAY 4

AN OLD FRIEND NAMED VIÑALES

The Morning Arrived Way Too Soon

Still feeling the afterglow from last night's extended adventures, I sat on the edge of the bed this morning craving a few precious moments before attempting to stand. Today, I needed an easy and relaxing day. For now, however, I was happy to settle for a quiet morning and a generous cup of strong Cuban coffee.

A few minutes later, my friends joined me in the hotel's lobby. After dazed greetings and can't-believe-its-already-morning smiles, we started a sluggish but determined march toward the Hotel Nacional's main restaurant in search of breakfast.

Once there, George and I unmercifully began to tease José about his rum-infused misadventures last night. Our friend, however, was not amused. He had absolutely no idea what we were talking about. He did not remember his search for the Tropicana Cabaret's bathrooms while inexplicably standing, inebriated, in the middle of the road outside the Tropicana Cabaret. He did not remember smuggling the rum-filled

Tropicana glass out of the cabaret or attempting to sneak it inside a private club either. As a matter of fact, he did not remember much about last night at all.

We had a great time last night; too bad José will never know.

After fueling on fried eggs, tropical fruit, a pitcher of water, and lots of Cuban coffee, my friends and I were finally ready to start the day. We made our way to the hotel's porte cochere and waited for Maidel to arrive.

Maidel, however, did not come alone to pick us up this morning. His hometown girlfriend from the city of Holguín was in the car with him and would be joining us on our planned visit to Viñales Valley today.

George, José, and I understood the situation. Maidel's oncologist girlfriend in Havana was the woman who owned Maidel's heart but would not give in to his romantic needs. His hometown girlfriend would. She was in town, and Maidel had a big smile painted on his face. Despite bloodshot eyes and a pale complexion, he seemed happy.

My friends and I walked towards Maidel's Chinese sedan with the dark-tinted windows and, after carefully evaluating how to best squeeze our bodies into his car, prepared to climb inside.

Like the previous three days, I sat in the front passenger seat next to Maidel. George, José, and Maidel's girlfriend-from-Holguín, however, struggled to fit their limbs and bodies into the car's space-limited rear seat. After a few awkward moments, they found a way to position their arms and legs to a bearable level of comfort and signaled their approval to begin the drive to Viñales.

Memories of My 1960 Cuba Farewell Tour

Looking out the passenger window at Havana's busy streets during our drive to Viñales Valley this morning, my mind wandered back to the days following my family's difficult decision to leave Cuba for a new life of exile in the United States.

One warm and sunny day in the fall of 1960, my father loaded our blue-and-white 1957 Ford and started to drive my grandmother Isabel, mother, brother, and me on a family road trip across the length of the island—wanting us to simultaneously discover and say goodbye to the country of our birth before we left. Our 1960 Cuba farewell tour first brought us west of Havana to Viñales Valley before changing course due east with stops at several coastal beaches, hamlets, and historical towns along the way. It culminated at the Basilica de la Caridad del Cobre in Santiago de Cuba, where we prayed for clarity, peace, and safety during our unpredictable future, as well as the lives of the loved ones we would soon be leaving behind and might never see again.

My parents hoped it would bring us some measure of peace and closure—sadly, it did not.

My family's 1960 Cuba farewell tour visit to Viñales Valley proved most memorable for me. That day, long ago, I arrived at the valley's rim with all the excitement and joy of a young child on vacation. It did not last long.

It was here, amid the valley's unique geological features and colorful foliage, that I first grew aware of the sadness that would surround my family and me throughout our trip. Not yet nine years old, the uncertainty of how my life would change at the conclusion of our farewell tour haunted me during my visit to Viñales Valley that day. Every time I thought about how I would soon be leaving my home, school, grandparents, uncles, aunts, and friends behind for an uncertain future in an unknown land, I felt fears and anxieties impossible for me to understand at my young age.

A shroud of sorrows blurred my view of the Viñales Valley floor on that clear and sunny day. My mother, sensing my discomfort and in pain herself, leaned toward me, kissed me on the cheek, and soothingly whispered, "Don't worry, Mayito, we will be all right. No matter what the future brings, we will always have one another." Sage words that always comforted me amid times of anguish during our last days in Cuba and early years of exile.

(Circa 1960) With my family and 1957 Ford on our Cuba Farewell Tour

Revisiting an Old Friend Named Viñales

Today, fifty-six years later, my parents and brother were with me in spirit as Maidel drove his girlfriend-from-Holguín, José, George, and me through Cuba's picturesque countryside toward Viñales Valley.

As soon as we left the city of Havana, the traffic on the highway dropped to just a few sporadic vehicles. Hundreds of persons walked along the side of the highway with their thumbs pointed upward, desperately trying to hitch a ride out of the hot Cuban sun. Many waited for buses while sitting on open-air wooden bus stop benches, sheltered only by their own umbrellas. Some shared the road with us on repurposed vintage trucks, tractors, and horse-drawn wooden carts used as taxis. Others traveled on horseback, bicycles, motorcycles, rusted vintage cars, and unrecognizable—almost-comical homemade vehicles.

The contrast between the beautiful western Cuba countryside gleaming under the day's clear skies—and the daily struggles of Cuban life here—provided for provocative, intriguing, and compelling images synonymous with the absurd contradictions that define the only reality most Cubans on the island have ever known.

No Shrouds of Sorrows Today

A couple of hours after leaving our hotel, my friends and I arrived at Viñales Valley and were welcomed by the sounds of the ever-present Cuban music played by the always-talented local musicians. We moved toward the brick railing along the rim of the valley and silently stared at the majestic view before us.

Fifty-six years ago, a shroud of sorrows obscured the magnificence of Viñales Valley from me. This morning, I had finally unveiled the beauty of an old friend I barely knew.

(May, 2016) Viñales Valley

The view of Viñales Valley from the visitor's platform terrace this morning extended to the horizon in all directions—it was a sight to behold. The amalgamation of the red soil visible between the flamboyant trees ablaze with color, the hundreds of royal palm trees softly swaying to the rhythm of the Cuban breeze, the tree-covered mogote geomorphological formations, and the traditional Cuban *bohio* (huts) dotting the valley floor below weaved a sight many artists attempt to capture on canvas, photography, poetry, and song.

None of them, however, will ever be able to fully express the natural beauty and richness of this intricate, balanced, and unspoiled natural habitat.

Reckless Abandon

Having absorbed the sights and sounds of Viñales Valley from atop its rim, my friends and I decided to also enjoy it from below. Maidel led us to a privately owned horse ranch on the valley floor and asked the owner to provide us with their most spirited and muscular horses to ride.

Once there, José, George, and I mounted our muscular beasts and started our equestrian exploration of the valley floor with a leisurely trot that eventually turned into a fun-filled, hair-blowing gallop in the open terrain.

The reckless abandon of riding these magnificent animals at full speed, the warmth of the Cuban sun on my face, and the power of the wind blowing through my hair, forced me to focus only on the moment. It was a beautiful and exhilarating experience.

For a delightful instant, I was young and invincible; I felt eternal and alive.

"Don't," I said to myself, "fall off this horse."

We galloped our horses toward a local farm where *campesinos* (farmers) raised pigs and harvested several crops, including *guayabitas*, a small guava berry indigenous only to this valley and used as the main ingredient of a sweet and potent local alcoholic beverage called *Guayabitas del Pinar*.

A few thrilling minutes later, we arrived—thirsty for a drink. George, José, and I sat with several of the *campesinos* inside one of their open-sided *bohios* and immediately started to share stories and savor the *guayabita* beverages we had heard so much about. Soon, we were toasting in Cuban brotherhood to anything and everything imaginable with our tasty alcoholic drinks. The more we drank, the more intimate our conversations became.

One of the farmers told us how earlier that day a horse ridden by a tourist was startled by one of their oversized pigs aimlessly roaming around the farm, throwing the severely sunburned rider, dressed all in white, headfirst into a red soil mud pit.

"You should have seen it," the farmer said.

"Seen what?" I asked.

"The color of the rider's red-stained clothing matched his skin," he deadpanned as everyone broke into laughter.

The Taste of Our Parents' Memory

Growing up in South Florida, I often heard my parents complain that American food lacked taste. The food in Cuba's countryside, they claimed, tasted better, was sweeter, and had more flavor. I discarded those statements as nostalgic longing for a Cuba they remembered and missed. After all, memories of the past are frequently idealized, and the smell and taste of foods and drinks are often heightened. George and José also remembered how their parents often said the same thing.

Soon, we would all find out if our parents were right.

My friends and I returned our no-nonsense domesticated beasts to their stables, joined Maidel and his girlfriend-from-Holguín inside his car, and started our drive toward a privately owned Paladar located on the rim of the valley above us.

The Paladar's open-sided dining room, large enough to sit about a hundred patrons, was mostly crowded with a local clientele that day. We claimed a picnic table with a great view of the valley below and prepared to order our lunch.

A few minutes later, a smiling waitress—dressed in traditional Cuban countryside attire—approached our table and informed us that there would be no menu to order from today. We would simply choose whatever we wanted to eat from family-style platters she would soon bring to our table. Hungry and tired, we smiled at the pretty waitress and waited for the platters of food to arrive.

Before we knew it, multiple plates of fresh organic food grown on neighboring farms and several pitchers of chilled local fruit drinks crowded our picnic table.

Everything we tried tasted out-of-this-world delicious. The pineapple juice was as sweet as lemonade. The *boniatos* (sweet potatoes) were rich and sweet. The chicken, potato, pork, rice, black beans, and sweet plantains truly had more flavor than their American counterparts—even those served at the best and most expensive Cuban restaurants in South Florida.

"Our parents," I said, "were right. Cuban food does have more flavor here."

My friends agreed.

A Lesson in American Civics and Tolerance

After we finished eating our lunch, George and I sipped on Cuban coffee and started to discuss American politics in Spanish. He defended one side of the political spectrum while I argued for the opposite. Two Cubans, however, even if they are from the United States, cannot discuss politics without passion. It did not take long before our political conversation started to reverberate from inside the suddenly quiet restaurant dining room.

Intoxicated by the delicious food we had just consumed, the sweet smells from the valley floor below, and the constant island breeze caressing our skins, George and I absentmindedly forgot that we were in Cuba, a land where political discourse other than praising the Castro regime was outlawed. Accustomed to the freedoms we took for granted in the United States, we did not think twice about the conversation we were having, oblivious to an audience that discretely and intently listened to every word we said.

Suddenly, things got uncomfortably interesting. A man sitting at an adjacent dining table stood up from his chair, pointed at us, and speaking to no one in particular but for all in the restaurant to hear, said in a rather elevated tone and volume, "Are all of you watching this?"

I felt the chill of finally realizing where I was and the incident George and I might have innocently started. My heart palpitated. George and I nervously looked at each other like two kids who knew they had broken the rules. We realized we should have known better.

"Listen to these two argue American politics—listen to them," the standing patron continued. "They don't agree on a single thing—nothing."

Then everything changed. The standing patron reflected for a minute, took a deep breath, extended his arms wide open, and proclaimed even louder, "Just watch, brothers. They will eventually agree to disagree and leave here as friends. Do you know why?" he announced rhetorically before concluding, "Because that is what real freedom sounds like."

The patron then looked at us, smiled, sat back in his chair, and continued to eat his lunch.

Incredibly, my friends and I, as well as everyone else in the restaurant that day, had just received a lesson—in communist Cuba no less—on the human right to free expression. I looked around the restaurant expecting an undercover government operative to walk toward us wanting to question our intentions, like the plainclothes agents who confronted me yesterday at the Anti-Imperialist Tribune. To my surprise, however, no one came. No one stirred. No one said anything. No one even looked at us.

The typical chatter and dish-clanging sounds, synonymous with restaurants everywhere, returned, and the patrons resumed eating their meals as if nothing had happened.

Pleasantly surprised that someone inside the restaurant had praised our unplanned exercise in American political discourse and civil liberties without creating an unfortunate incident, I looked at my friends and smiled with great satisfaction. I was proud that the Cubans who listened to their fellow countryman's surprising appraisal of our conversation displayed a level of tolerance not expected in Cuba and accepted his observations without any act of repression.

The patron who delivered his analysis of our political discussion will never know it, but his oratory that day filled me with a sense of profound humility and great hope for Cuba's future. I looked at the patron and smiled back.

My friends and I left the Paladar and headed toward Maidel's car, walking past a modest house with a sign outside its front porch that read *"Presidente del CDR"* (President of the Committee for the Defense of the Revolution). This "president's" sole responsibility is to know what the neighbors are doing, planning, or saying and report those behaving suspiciously to the authorities.

Because of this, Cubans all over the island are careful of what they say in public and whom they are seen with. A CDR accusation could lead to government detention, interrogation, or worse. It could also lead to punishments ranging from the loss of food rations to incarceration.

We were fortunate the *Presidente del CDR* was not in the restaurant with us today.

Once we got to his car, Maidel announced that he wanted to show us *La Cueva del Indio*, a nearby cave located inside one of the mogote formations surrounding Viñales Valley. Maidel, José, George, Maidel's girlfriend-from-Holguín, and I somehow managed to squeeze our newly food-enhanced bodies and limbs back inside the Chinese sedan with the very dark-tinted windows and started the short drive there.

Driving through Pinar Del Río's countryside on our way to the cave this afternoon was a soothing and memorable experience. Its pastoral country roads weave bucolically around colorful farms and open terrain dotted with hundreds of majestic royal palm trees, dozens of steep-sided mogotes, and magnificent mature forests.

Halfway to the cave, however, we slowly disentangled our limbs and squeezed out of the car, wanting to visit a huge bar called *Palenque de los Cimarrones*—built inside a voluminous natural void on the side of one of the mogotes surrounding Viñales Valley. Normally, we would have made our presence felt in this impressive watering hole, but last night's quantity of Cuban rum consumption, three days of sleep deprivation, and today's overindulgence of *Guayabitas Del Pinar* alcoholic drinks and Cuban food made it impossible for us to give in to our egos and testosterone impulses.

There would be no drinking alcohol at *Palenque* this afternoon—a tall glass of cold lemonade would have to do.

Floating Underground

We eventually arrived at the *Cueva del Indio* cave and safely made our way around the mature oxen and menacing bulls that habitually graze in front of its ancient wooden ticket booth. We entered the cave through a small unmarked entrance on the side of the mogote and immediately found ourselves on a dimly lit pathway leading to its cavernous main chamber, defined by impressive natural formations, including dozens of stalagmites and stalactites.

The cave's main chamber's lighting, even though amateurish by international standards, still worked well. The simple white lighting honestly emphasized the brutal natural forces that formed this magnificent space of geological beauty without the themed enhancements and theatrical distortions typical of most commercial cave lighting around the world today. As a result, the impressive cave's features looked real.

From the cave's main chamber, a trail took us to a natural staircase descending onto an underground river, where a guide awaited to take us on a floating tour of the cave's natural underground formations.

Once there, my friends and I settled into the guide's wooden rowboat and started our exploration of the cave's underground river chambers. Now and then, the rowboat's operator would stop rowing, aim his simple flashlight at predetermined natural highlights, and explain the geological features that formed the subterranean walls and roof of the cave's impressive interior.

Our low-tech floating tour was definitely not a Disney World production; it was, however, an honest and effective exploration of the cave without the dramatic enhancements that so often transforms natural beauty into a theatrical show.

The underground river eventually exited the cave, taking us to a disembarkation zone before once again disappearing below ground.

(May, 2016) La Cueva del Indio

By the time we exited the cave, nighttime had descended on Viñales and we decided to start the slow and dangerous drive back to Havana.

With few streetlights lighting Cuba's countryside roads, only the headlights of our car illuminated the pitch-black rural streets we found ourselves trying to safely navigate through. Maidel nervously maneuvered, ever so slowly, around the many pedestrians, horseback riders, homemade buggies, and horse-drawn carts without taillights attempting to share the dark roadways with us tonight.

There was little, if any, conversation in the car during the drive back to Havana. All eyes were on the road ahead of us in a collective effort to help Maidel avoid a tragedy.

A couple of tense hours later, just a few blocks from the Hotel Nacional, my mind drifted one more time to my previous visit to Viñales Valley during my family's farewell tour of Cuba in 1960. That day, facing family separation and an unpredictable future in exile, I had clouds in my eyes and a shroud over my heart.

There were no clouds or shrouds at Viñales today—there were no moments of sadness, sorrows, anxieties, or fear. Today had been a most welcomed day of cleansing emotions, living in the moment, and reckless abandon. I had finally unveiled the face of an old friend, made peace with my past, and replaced the uncertainty of long ago with the acceptance, love, and hope that so far defined my return to the land I hoped to rediscover.

The last time I visited Viñales Valley, I was saying goodbye. Today, I simply said hello.

(May, 2016) Horseback riding on the Viñales Valley floor

DAY 5

"I AM A MATEO TOO"

Memories of Beach Days and Sugarcane

When I lived in Cuba, my family and I would often climb into our car, drive to the beach at Santa Maria del Mar, and check into the former *Club de Contadores Publico* (Accountant's Club) for a weekend of sand, surf, and fun.

Once there, my parents would spend their time swimming; enjoying a game of cards with friends; trying their luck at bingo; and playing softball, baseball, tennis, or squash for bragging rights. My friends at the club and I would hang out at the beach, play baseball, and entertain ourselves with unscripted and unsupervised games. Sometimes we would ambush unsuspecting crabs and use them to scare our other friends tanning on the beach.

At night, my family and I would eat at the club's restaurant and watch a movie inside the theater room before my parents sent my brother and me to bed, preferring to spend the rest of their evening drinking and dancing under the stars or strolling along the club's romantic beachfront boardwalk as a couple.

We would often combine our trips to Santa Maria del Mar with Sunday visits to my great-aunts' home in the nearby town of Hershey, American chocolatier Milton Hershey's flagship town in Cuba. This master planned town, completed in 1918, was the place where Mr. Hershey planted, harvested, and refined the sugar he used for making his famous chocolates in Pennsylvania.

The town of Hershey eventually grew to be over sixty thousand acres with five raw sugar mills, four electrical plants, hundreds of homes for sale or rent, three schools, golf course, baseball stadium, hotel, and town square. My mother grew up living there with her parents, brothers, and extended family during the 1920s-1930s, while my grandfather worked as the director of the Hershey Railroad Terminal.

Once my grandfather was promoted to assume a similar position at the larger (and busier) Casablanca Railroad Station in Havana, he moved his family from the town of Hershey to the nation's capital. My great-aunts, however, chose to remain in Hershey, where they continued to live and work for the rest of their lives.

My Sunday visits to the town of Hershey were always fun. The slow-paced country lifestyle was very different from Havana's urban life, providing me with an interminable rural setting to discover and play in.

The highlight of my weekend visits there usually consisted of running with the local children behind the farmers transporting the sugar harvest from the fields to the mills atop their oxen-pulled wooden carts—screaming at the top of our lungs until the drivers threw sugarcane off their wagons for us to enjoy. With a stalk of sugarcane safely in hand, I would run to my great-aunts' shaded porch and give it to my grandfather to peel with his knife. Once he was done, I would sit on the swing hanging from the porch's rafters and chew on the cane's raw sugar.

Today, I wanted to retrace our family weekend outings by visiting Santa Maria del Mar in the morning and the town of Hershey during the afternoon—before ending the day in Varadero Beach.

New Day — New Surprises

Maidel and his girlfriend-from-Holguín, arrived under the Hotel Nacional's porte-cochere to pick up my friends and me this morning, and soon we were off on the day's adventures.

The drive to Santa Maria del Mar from Havana this morning was as beautiful as it was relaxing. One of the benefits to tourists visiting Cuba today is the low volume of traffic on the highways once you leave the urban areas. Thirty minutes after leaving our hotel in Havana, my friends and I found ourselves alone on the road, driving through central Cuba's lush rural countryside.

Before we knew it, we reached an especially delightful stretch of the highway highlighted by dozens of pineapple plantations and countless groves of royal palm trees. I remembered this part of the drive well— soon, we would be leaving the main highway toward the beaches of Santa Maria Del Mar.

The same rush of anticipation I always felt as a child whenever my family and I reached this part of the trip during our beach outings returned this morning. In a few minutes, we would be arriving at the place of my Cuban childhood synonymous with sand, surf, and fun!

Sand, Surf, Crabs, and Dining Under the Stars

The approach from the highway toward the beaches of Santa Maria del Mar was exactly the way I always visualized it. Once we arrived to the access road leading to the beachfront resorts and hotels, my internal directional system took over. Somehow I remembered the location of the former Accountant's Club and led Maidel to it. Within minutes, I was back visiting another old friend.

We found a parking spot, stepped out of the car, and started walking toward the hotel's lobby entrance.

"How did you know where the old Accountant's Club was?" George asked.

"Every nine-year-old child remembers their way to the beach," I responded. "Don't you?"

I expected the former Accountant's Club to be exactly the way I left it. After all, every place I had visited in Havana thus far remained in a time warp. I was wrong. A foreign investor had purchased the property several years ago and renovated it into the present-day Hotel Atlantico. The developer's renovations, however, had fortunately left the club's vintage exterior facades mostly unchanged, allowing me to recognize them as soon as we arrived.

My friends and I walked through the hotel's lobby and immediately headed toward the beach area beyond. Once there, George and José settled under a beachfront tiki bar to order some drinks and drool over the bikini-clad tourists bronzing their bodies on the silky white sand. I decided, instead, to go for a walk along the shoreline in search of any memory that would help me remember my weekends here as a child.

It was good to see that the ocean, where I spent a substantial portion of my time during my childhood visits here, was still as turquoise blue as I always thought it was. Its reflections of the bright morning sunlight seemed to welcome me back today with the glimmer of a million points of light. I recalled playing with my childhood friends here once, dunking our heads and one another under its surface for fun while screaming with delight. Much to my amusement, even the rocky beach area where I would carefully ambush those poor unsuspecting side-crawling crabs to scare my friends tanning on the beach was still there as well.

I couldn't help but smile at the memory of those innocent, carefree days.

José, George, and I eventually left the sand and walked back into the hotel complex from its beach entry gate. From that vantage point, it was easy to see that the developer's renovations of the former Accountant's Club were limited only to minor additions and modernization efforts throughout the resort.

Fortunately for me, the hotel room wing where my family and I would stay during our weekend visits here and the exquisite "under the stars" cabaret, defined by its iconic 1950s modernist slim profile concrete vaults, had somehow remained mostly unchanged. Only the vintage granite *CCP* floor logo was gone— replaced by a new pool built in its place.

Memories of the men and women I remembered dining and dancing in the "under the stars" cabaret, dressed in the elegant clothing of the 1950s, returned easily. They would strut through the open-air sitting area with their daiquiri or Cuba libre drinks in hand, putting them down only to dance to the unmistakable music of the era. Delicious meals, pulsating music, incessant conversations, and laughter once filled this place with unabashed joy. I could almost hear my father's unmistakable raspy voice as he told his stories and joked with friends.

If only for a few seconds, I not only saw the old *Club de Contadores Publico* this morning but felt it as well. It brought a big smile to my face.

My Perfect World Inside the White Foul Lines

Unfortunately, the baseball field where I often played in organized and impromptu games with my friends was sadly neglected. I looked at the ballfield this morning and thought about all the fun I had there once. I remembered how, in addition to playing baseball games with kids my age, I was allowed to shag fly balls in the outfield whenever the adults took batting practice. Afterward, I would stay and field countless ground balls on the clay infield off the bat of ex-major leaguer and club director Roberto Ortiz, earning much praise for my efforts. Sometimes the adults would even allow me to play with them in their highly competitive games.

Every time I stepped over the perfectly straight white foul lines defining this baseball field, the world seemed perfect. Today, I remembered just how perfect it really was.

It was sad saying goodbye to Santa Maria del Mar, but the morning was quickly turning into the afternoon, and we had to start our drive to the town of Hershey.

My friends and I squeezed ourselves back into Maidel's car and set out to find the second half of my family weekend getaways.

(May, 2016) The former Club de Contadores Publicos' Under the Stars Cabaret

The Town that Milton Hershey Built

I grew excited at the thought of returning to the town of Hershey today. It was always a place of great fun and exhilarating adventures for me.

This afternoon, I wanted to visit the addresses of the homes where my mother grew up and my great-aunts lived. Since my mother, at ninety-three years of age, was too frail to accompany me on my trip to Cuba, I wanted to surprise her with photographs of those places I knew she would remember, especially from her childhood days here. I hoped it would bring her great pleasure.

The approximately twenty-minute drive from Santa Maria del Mar to the town of Hershey took us through a lush landscape and hilly countryside I did not recognize or remember.

Once my friends and I arrived at the edge of town, we were unexpectedly greeted by a rather large billboard announcing the entrance to the town of Camilo Cienfuegos—a revolutionary name no one in the town of Hershey has the patience for or acknowledges. As a result, the "Cienfuegos" billboard was uncared for, worn, and dilapidated. The much smaller "Hershey" sign, next to the railroad station, was freshly painted and well maintained.

It was good to see that the people living here still cared for the legacy and goodwill of Milton Hershey and the town he built.

We stopped and briefly left our car to admire and photograph the ancient Hershey Railroad Station, where my grandfather once worked as its director. I peeked through the station's windows and imagined my grandfather working there as a young man while my mother and uncles attended school nearby.

It was a great way to start my return visit to the town that meant so much to my Mateo family.

After taking a few photographs of the railroad station, my friends and I returned to Maidel's car and prepared to start our search for the homes I came here hoping to find. Before we could drive out of the station's parking lot, however, a well-dressed older man unexpectedly walked up to our car and tapped on the front passenger door next to where I sat.

Momentarily startled, I lowered the car window and asked him, "May I help you?"

"You guys look like you are lost," our unanticipated visitor said. "Would you like me to help you find what you came here looking for?"

"Sure," I responded, not really thinking about how we would best fit him inside our already-crowded car.

A Town of Faded Shadows

With Maidel's girlfriend-from-Holguín uncomfortably seated on top of our new guide's lap and squeezed between George and José on the rear bench seat of our ominous black Chinese sedan, we started our drive into town.

Driving through Hershey's industrial and commercial sectors toward its residential district this afternoon highlighted the sad truth that this once-prosperous sugar-producing town had unfortunately become a faded shadow of its former self. Sugarcane was no longer harvested here, and most of the sugar mills and smokestacks had either collapsed or been demolished. Those still partially standing looked like they were abandoned decades ago—their worn shells and shattered windows creating an eerie vision of what once was the iconic symbol of this innovative and productive master planned town. Only a portion of the rusting electric plant still remained; its power production rerouted toward Havana long ago.

The Town Square's clinic, convenience store, and pharmacy were closed and shuttered. Inside the square's food store (the only shop still open in town), most of the shelves sat empty and dusty. The golf course and baseball fields had become unkempt, weed-filled, grassy lots and the partially collapsed Social Center was barely visible behind its overgrown vegetation.

The Hershey Hotel's stone exterior walls were all that remained of this once-elegant building; the roof having succumbed to the elements years ago and its interior partitions, electrical infrastructure, and plumbing fixtures reclaimed by Hershey's residents over the years in desperate attempts to maintain their homes. Even the concrete sidewalks were gone now, having been repurposed as repair material by the town's residents as well.

The once-proud town of Hershey, unfortunately, continues to crumble a little more each day, cannibalized out of necessity by its own residents in order to survive Cuba's failed economic system and the ravages of time.

Few people work in the town of Hershey today. The only jobs left are associated with the repurposed electrical plant and the seldom-used railway station. Those fortunate enough to be employed earn the equivalent of only twenty to thirty dollars a month. Those who are not, just sit on the courtyard benches of the otherwise-abandoned Town Square and stare out into nowhere.

Regrettably, a sad and palpable sense of hopelessness shrouds the town of Hershey today.

Searching Against All Odds

With the help of our unanticipated guide, we eventually arrived to Hershey's residential sector and started searching for street signs that would help us find the locations of the two homes I came here looking for.

The few concrete street monument signs we found, however, were unfortunately completely eroded, and most of the homes we drove past were missing their house numbers. We were the only vehicle on the road, and no one was walking on the streets or sidewalks next to us.

It would be nearly impossible, I thought, to find the addresses I came looking for in a town without street signs, house numbers, and no one around to ask for directions.

The only hope left was to find an elderly person who had always lived in the town of Hershey and might remember the locations of the two homes my family lived in nearly eighty years ago.

I asked Maidel to drive slow enough to allow me the time to look through the windows of every home we passed for someone who matched this description. Even though it might have seemed like an improbable task, I thought, it was certainly not impossible.

José and George thought I was at best overly optimistic, at worst just downright crazy. Several times, I almost gave up my search. I'm glad I did not.

As planned, Maidel drove agonizingly slow through the streets of Hershey while I scanned the windows of every home we passed, hoping for a most improbable moment.

A few minutes later, I caught a glimpse of a slim and elderly woman slumped over an old wooden wheelchair looking down at the floor of her partially screened front porch.

I asked Maidel to stop the car, took a deep breath of hope, left the vehicle, and slowly walked toward her while flashing my friendliest I-am-not-a-dubious-stranger smile.

"Good morning," I said.

"Good morning," she responded. "May I help you?"

"I am looking for the home where the Marcos Mateo family lived during the 1920s and 1930s," I explained.

"Why on earth would you want to know where Marcos Mateo lived so long ago?" the elderly lady asked with an intrigued look on her time-worn face.

"Because I am his grandson," I continued.

The nonagenarian woman straightened herself in her wheelchair, thought for a moment, smiled broadly at me, and said, "Dear God, are you Mayito?"

I gulped, and a cold chill ran through my spine. "Yes, I am," I responded. "I am Mario Cartaya Mateo."

"My name is Armenia Mateo," she said. "I am a Mateo too! I am your great-aunt."

I could not believe what had just happened! What were the odds that the only person I saw and approached as we randomly drove down the streets of the town of Hershey turned out to be a family member I never knew existed?

Hearing our conversation on the front porch, a younger woman walked out of the house to check in on the elderly lady and the unexpected stranger she was talking with. Once she noticed our relaxed expressions and demeanor, the younger woman looked curiously at me, smiled, and said, "Good afternoon, I'm Clara Mateo Diaz. Armenia is my aunt."

Armenia, still slumped in her wheelchair, smiled at her niece and said, "Clara, meet your cousin, Mayito."

I stood in front of Armenia's front porch speechless, overwhelmed by this most remarkable moment. Maidel looked dumbfounded. José could not stop laughing and shaking his head in disbelief. George just looked at me in bewildered amazement, took a deep breath, and said, "Mario, you need to stay here with your family awhile."

He was right. All these years, I did not think I had any family members left living in Cuba. It turned out I was wrong. I had found the last of the Mateos in the town of Hershey, and we had a lot to talk about.

Maidel offered to drive our unanticipated guide home and then take his girlfriend-from-Holguín, George, and José to Varadero Beach before returning to pick me up later this afternoon. This, he said, would allow me the time and privacy to bond and get acquainted with my newly discovered family. I watched my friends leave and resumed my unanticipated family reunion.

I sat inside the front porch with Armenia and Clara wanting to ask a thousand questions but unsure where to start. Armenia looked at me with a soft expression on her face, smiled again, and asked, "How is your mother, Leida?"

"My mother is doing well," I said. "She is like you, elderly but with a clear and sharp mind."

Armenia paused for a moment, looked down at her swollen ankles, and said, "Your mother was so beautiful, you know. She was blonde, slim, and played the piano like an angel—a piano your grandfather built for her. It was a wonderful instrument."

I started to laugh. My mother always reminisced with visible pride how my grandfather built her first piano as a birthday gift when she was a little girl living in the town of Hershey. I halfway believed her. I mean, who builds a piano as a gift? Obviously, my grandfather did; Armenia had just confirmed it.

Armenia smiled again, and her aged eyes twinkled with a beautiful childish innocence that took me by surprise. She peppered me with countless stories about the times she played dolls with my mother and all the fun they shared as little girls growing up here. She knew about my Mateo grandparents' and uncle Miguel's deaths in Havana and wanted to know everything about my life and family in the United States. She told me how much my grandfather, Marcos, was loved by her friends and how he would decorate not just their homes but also the streets of the town of Hershey during the Christmas holidays.

A Promise Kept

After a long and insightful conversation about our family's history, Clara offered to walk me to the house where my grandparents raised my mother and uncles long ago.

Once there, she introduced me as her cousin from Miami to the home's current residents and convinced them to allow her to give me a tour of the house where my mother spent the earliest years of her childhood. I did not know this place, but it was great fun to imagine my mother and mischievous uncles living here as children, playing and teasing one another while my grandfather worked at the nearby Hershey Train Station.

This was the home I promised my elderly mother I would try to find and photograph for her. Somehow, against all odds, I had found it.

After taking my pictures, the house where my mother grew up remained where it had always been; the photographs I took, however, came back with me to Fort Lauderdale. They made my mother very happy.

(Circa 1931) From left to right: My Uncle Miguel, mother Leida and Uncle Marcolin growing up in the town of Hershey

Clara and I left my mother's childhood home and walked a few blocks toward the house where my other great-aunts—Mita, Tete, and Amparo—once lived. This was the home I would often visit with my parents on our weekend return trips from Santa Maria del Mar and would sit on its porch to chew on my well-earned sugarcane.

I did not recognize the elderly lady who lived there now, but astonishingly, she remembered me well.

"Mayito," she said, "do you remember this house?"

"Yes," I said, "this is where my great-aunts once lived, and I would often visit on Sundays."

"Don't forget your great-uncle Geromito," she interjected.

She was right; he lived here briefly too. I had almost forgotten.

She led me through the unchanged interiors of the house I grew to remember with every step we took inside its walls and then walked me back to the front porch wanting to continue exchanging stories with me.

"I remember sitting on this porch to chew on sugarcane every time my family and I came to visit my great-aunts here," I said.

"Yes, Mayito, you would chew on your sugarcane right here," she said and pointed to a freshly painted ancient wood swing hanging from the old and worn roof rafters.

I couldn't believe the darn thing was still there!

"You, along with the other kids, would run after the farmers carrying the sugar harvest on their oxen-pulled carts from the fields to the mills. None of you would stop screaming until the farmers tossed you stalks of sugarcane from atop their carts," she continued. "You would bring your sugarcane here, and your grandfather would peel them for you to chew on while sitting on this very swing. You were always so happy here!"

"Yes, I was," I answered in a soft whisper.

That old wooden swing, still supported from the roof structure above my great-aunt's former porch, once formed the background of my most beautiful memories from my weekend visits to the town of Hershey during the 1950s. Incredibly, it was at least sixty years old and still in use.

I sat on the freshly painted vintage wooden swing still hanging in the same place it had always been and thought about my childhood days of sugar once spent here. This time, however, there was no sugarcane to chew on, just beautiful memories to remember.

An Unplanned Family Reunion

I asked Clara if I could take her to lunch. She laughed and said there were no restaurants in or near Hershey anymore. She had, however, already arranged for her family to have lunch with me at her home. By the time we returned to her house, everyone was already there.

After lots of hugs and never-ending conversations, Armenia; Clara; her husband, Marcelo; their son, Angel; and I sat down to eat.

Clara apologized for not having any meat to eat. Her family, she said, had not eaten red meat in over thirty years, not because of any dietary restriction but rather as a result of not finding meat for sale or barter. We ate a lunch prepared from the black beans and rice she picked up with her monthly government ration card, the eggs she got from the chickens she kept in her backyard, and the *boniato* (sweet potato) and greens she grew in her garden. We had orange juice from the oranges off her trees and enjoyed a flan made by her from the milk she routinely bartered with friends in return for homegrown green vegetables from her garden.

This, she explained, had been her way of life for decades. She told me that country people in Cuba, because they have gardens and chickens, eat better than the urban dwellers in Havana.

During lunch, Marcelo informed me that ever since my grandfather left the town of Hershey to work at Havana's

Casablanca Railroad Station in the late 1930s, all the directors for the Hershey Railroad Station had been Mateo family members. Presently, his son, Angel, was the director. Marcelo was very proud of Angel and the Mateo legacy here.

Interestingly enough, by now, so was I.

We continued to talk about our family, toasted with a glass of water to the Mateo legacy, and celebrated a beautiful and poignant family reunion, decades in the making.

The love of family surrounding us this afternoon was real and palpable. Through it all, I could not stop thinking about my grandparents, uncles, mother, father, and older brother.

I wished they could have been here with us today.

Leaving My Newfound Family

Soon, the sun started to set on what had been another improbable day in Cuba, and Maidel arrived to pick me up. It was time to leave the town of Hershey and rejoin my friends already in Varadero Beach.

Saying goodbye to my newfound Mateo family was not easy. We hugged one another with bittersweet tears in our eyes and promised to stay in touch.

Everyone asked me to give their love to my mother in the United States. I could not wait to tell her the story of our beautiful unanticipated family reunion.

I hesitantly climbed into Maidel's car, waved goodbye to my rediscovered family, and prepared myself to leave them again.

(May, 2016) With my newfound family in the Town of Hershey

Sweet Days of Sugar

Maidel had already started our drive away from Hershey on one of the town's deserted and dusty country roads when we came upon a most remarkable sight.

I asked Maidel to quickly stop his black Chinese sedan, now covered with a thick layer of light-grey dust, stepped out of the car, and started to walk on the gravel road toward the shadowy silhouette of an elderly man sitting motionless atop an ancient wood sugar cart pulled by two large oxen. Behind him, two cows stood inexplicably roped to the cart.

The old farmer watched me walk toward him and grinned widely as I approached. The closer I got, the more I stared in disbelief. He seemed, at first, like a ghostly vision out of my childhood—a distant memory of the town of Hershey's sugar farming past—resurrected in the flesh.

I soon found out, however, that he was all too real.

"Good afternoon," I called out.

"Good afternoon," he responded.

"That's a beautiful ox-pulled wooden cart you are sitting on," I said. "How long have you had it?"

"About sixty years," he said. "I used to carry sugarcane in it long ago, when there was a sugar crop here. Now, however, I use it as a taxi, taking people from the town of Hershey to neighboring villages."

"Did you ever throw sugarcane from atop your cart for the local kids to chew on?" I asked.

"Yes, but that was many years ago," he sighed. "Why do you ask? Were you one of those kids that used to run behind my cart screaming at me?"

"Yes, I was," I responded almost apologetically.

The implausible had found me one more time today! Astonishingly, I was having a conversation with a most surreal figure of a time long ago: an elderly farmer who unknowingly framed the most memorable images from my visits to the town of Hershey when I was a young boy. I could hardly believe the serendipity of the moment.

I calmed myself down, took a deep breath, smiled with deep appreciation at this most unanticipated surprise, and asked him the question that had piqued my curiosity from the moment I first saw him, "Do you pull those two cows with you everywhere you go?"

"I can see you are not from here," he responded with a wink and a smile. "If I left them at home, someone would steal them ... and eat them!"

The elderly man was no ghost. Even though the octogenarian sugar farmer was once an integral part of my childhood days in the town of Hershey, he was still busy living his present—courageously surviving his Cuban reality one day at a time by supplementing his meager monthly state income with a repurposed oxen-pulled sugar cart he now used as a taxicab. Even at his advanced age, he was managing to maintain a degree of self-sufficiency and pride undeniably visible in his smiling eyes.

We walked toward each other and shook hands.

"Thank you for once spoiling us kids with your sugarcane," I said. "You were the highlight of my visits here when I was a child."

"*Oye*," he said, "I miss the sweet days of sugarcane. I even miss you screaming kids. It was a time of great fun. Thank you for spending time with me this afternoon."

His wrinkled, ancient eyes twinkled once more and his timeworn lips slowly curled into a most appreciative smile. I smiled back, thanked him again, and climbed back into the Chinese sedan's passenger seat.

Maidel and I looked at each other and laughed. No words were necessary to explain my visit to the town of Hershey today. The knowledge of the astonishing events that welcomed me here sufficed. I felt humbled and thankful for my good fortune.

We waved a sad goodbye to the old sugar farmer and resumed our drive to Varadero Beach.

(May, 2016) The old sugar farmer, vintage sugar cart repurposed as a taxi, oxen, and cows.

Return to Yumuri Valley

The drive to Varadero Beach on the Via Blanca highway took us above and through Yumuri Valley, a vast and beautiful nature reserve stretching from the mountains of central Cuba to the turquoise-blue ocean defining the island's northern coast.

The Via Blanca crosses Yumuri Valley at the Bacunayagua Bridge, an impressive structure known for its scenic visitor's center. With scenery too beautiful to miss, Maidel and I parked the car, climbed the steps leading to the viewing platform, and spent the next few minutes enjoying the view of the majestic valley below us.

Hundreds of thousands of Cuban royal palm trees and millions of tropical plants covered the impressive valley floor today, highlighted by the red hues of the early evening's setting sun. I remembered coming to this very same viewing platform during my family's farewell to Cuba trip in 1960, shortly before we immigrated to the United States. Today, the valley still looked as green and vast as I always pictured it.

It was a thrill returning to Yumuri Valley again.

By the time Maidel and I arrived at the Hotel Paradisus Varadero Beach Resort, it was well after dark. George had already checked me into the hotel, and my bags were waiting for me inside my guest room.

After checking in at the hotel's reception desk, I walked into my room, took a long shower, got dressed, wandered over to George's room, and knocked on his door—ready to have dinner and investigate the Varadero nightlife.

Hungry and tired, George, José, and I started making our way through the perfectly manicured five-star resort's gardens toward the hotel's upscale Japanese restaurant where my friends had already made dinner reservations for the three of us.

Once there, we ordered dinner, feasted on a great meal prepared by a talented chef on a hibachi grill built into our table, and then decided to stay in our seats, wanting to enjoy some after-dinner drinks and conversation.

I mentioned to my friends how odd it was that today was May 20, Cuban Independence Day from Spain, and no one seemed to be celebrating it. As a matter of fact, I said, we had not noticed any announcements, media events, flags, banners, or billboards marking this important date.

The Waitress and the Palooka

Our waitress, who had been friendly and engaging throughout dinner, brought us a new round of drinks. Still confused about the lack of public acknowledgment of this historical date, I innocently asked her, "Do you know today's date?"

"May the 20th," the waitress responded.

"Do you know what it represents?" I asked.

"Today is just like any other day," she said, shrugging her shoulders.

"Are you proud of being Cuban?" I innocently pried.

"Of course," she answered and looked away from me in disgust.

"Well, today is the day Cuba became a sovereign nation," I offered naively. "It's Cuba's Independence Day."

I honestly did not say that to upset her. I truly believed she might have not been aware of the significance of today's date.

She glared at me with a look I struggled to understand, turned to face me, squared her slim shoulders, and defiantly responded with a stressed tone loud enough for all the restaurant patrons to hear, "That's what you imperialists say, but it's not true because in 1902, Cuba just switched colonial occupation from Spain to America. Cuba's real Independence Day is January 1, 1959, the day Fidel Castro liberated us!"

I was stunned. Unknowingly, I had opened a door that was taboo and placed the waitress, my friends, and me in serious jeopardy.

Cuban students, I learned later, have been taught this warped historical alternate truth for years. Celebrating May 20 as Cuba's Independence Day is prohibited by the Cuban government today and considered a counterrevolutionary activity. Those caught celebrating May 20 as Cuban Independence Day could find themselves being detained, interrogated, or worse.

The waitress left all upset and never came back.

In her place, two oversized men came to visit us. One brought the dinner bill, which I assigned to my room. The other, a big palooka-looking brute, pretended to clean the hibachi grill built into our dining table even though our cook had already polished it to a shine.

Palooka was a bad actor. It was obvious that he was an undercover security guard sent to watch us, listen in on our conversation, and evaluate our intentions. By now, however, the topic of our discussion had changed. The more we drank, shared stories, and laughed, the more uncomfortable he became. You could see his growing frustration with every story we told and joke we shared.

Eventually, Palooka looked at me with a scowl on his face and growled, "You are really old."

"Maybe I am," I said, trying to defend my honor, "but at least I have hair. You, on the other hand, are old ... and bald!"

Fortunately, Palooka did not answer.

This was the second time this week that an undercover Cuban security guard grew irritable with me and called me *old*. Perhaps it was a standard Cuban security guard intimidation tactic ... or maybe they just wanted to hurt my feelings.

It did not work.

After my moment of male bravado faded, my friends and I knew that our time at the resort's Japanese restaurant had come to an end. George, José, and I waved goodbye to Mr. Palooka and took the first taxi we found to one of the several nightclubs nearby.

Letting Lose in Varadero Beach

The unmistakable sound of Cuban music and anticipation of a night out filled the nighttime air as our taxi pulled up in front of the nearest nightclub's front door. We entered the smoky and crowded building and settled in for a night of letting loose.

The place was small and primitive by Miami South Beach standards but alive with delicious salsa and reggaeton music delivered by a talented and engaging Cuban band from atop a raised wooden stage. Adjacent to the stage was a dance floor overflowing with mostly South American tourists dancing and moving suggestively to the contagious rhythm and pulsating beat that infused the night. Beyond the dance floor, dozens of tables hosted groups and couples drinking, talking, and singing in concert with the songs being played by the band.

George, José, and I stood in front of a rather large sit-down bar at the rear of the club—surrounded by scores of inebriated guests mingling, drinking, and dancing all around us—and prepared to let loose.

I ordered the first of several glasses of Havana Club and surrendered to the night's charged atmosphere. I drank to my childhood in Havana; I drank to growing up in Miami; I drank to my newfound family in the town of Hershey; I drank to the inexplicable events that had defined my journey to Cuba thus far;

I drank to *El Cambio*; I drank to the US; I drank to my friends—and I drank to the Florida Gators!

I did not drink to Palooka or Popeye and his comrades ... but I did drink to my drink.

This went on all night! You get the picture? Nothing was going to wipe the goofy smile off my face.

Finally, in the early hours of the morning, my friends and I flagged another taxi and headed back to the hotel. It was time to call it a night.

Today had been another incredible day in Cuba. I felt so satisfied and grateful. I felt so alive. I also felt the cumulative effect of every drink I had consumed.

Around four in the morning, I somehow found my room, opened the door, crawled into bed, puffed up my pillow, and fell soundly asleep.

(May, 2016) Varadero Beach—closest point in Cuba to the United States

DAY 6

THE PELICAN

A Lazy Day at the Beach

Five emotional days in Cuba and an equal number of nights fueled by Cuban Rum and little sleep had finally taken their toll on my friends and me. Last night was the tipping point.

I slept late this morning—very late. I looked at the dated windup alarm clock on the nightstand next to me and noticed it was almost noon. Determined to start the day, I jumped out of bed, took an extra-long shower, mustered the strength to wiggle my bathing suit into place, walked over to George's room, and knocked on his door.

He opened it still wearing his pajamas; looked at me with tired, half-opened eyes; and said, "Dude, what time is it?"

"It's almost noon," I said. "You need to get dressed. Varadero Beach is waiting for us."

"Okay, okay, just give me a few minutes," George muttered in obvious discomfort.

"Sure, man. Have you heard from José this morning?" I asked.

"I called his room several times, brother, but he is not answering," he said. "I don't think he is doing so well this morning."

"You don't look so good either," I said.

"Well, neither do you," he retorted and started to laugh.

A few minutes later, George stepped outside his room with his hair brushed meticulously into place, his bathing suit on, and ready to start the day. Still concerned about our friend's condition this morning, George and I walked over to José's room and pounded on his door—hoping he would answer it.

A pale José peeked out of his room, winced, and painfully moaned, "You guys look hungover. What the hell do you want?"

"It's past noon," I said. "Let's go get some coffee!"

"Is that all you want?" he asked and disappeared inside his room to finish getting dressed and washing his face.

Once José finished his beach morning ritual, he agonizingly slid out of his room and joined George and me on a most deliberate walk in search of the first restaurant we could find serving Cuban coffee. Within minutes, we found the perfect place.

We sat at the first available table and proceeded to reclaim a little of our lost energy.

For the first time this week, I had nothing planned for the day. Other than visiting Varadero a couple of times with my family when I was a little boy, I had no prior history with this place. There was no past for me to rediscover here. The time had finally come for me to enjoy a well-earned day of mental and physical relaxation. I was ready to enjoy Cuba like the many tourists who had surrounded me all week.

I wanted today to be no more than just a lazy day at the beach with my friends.

(Circa 1957) With my older brother in Varadero Beach

Growing up in Miami, I would often hear my parents reminisce about the beauty of Varadero Beach. They would unequivocally describe it as the most beautiful beach on the planet. My father would often say that in Varadero Beach, he could walk a half-mile into the sea and still be surrounded by chest-high warm and clear turquoise-blue water. The sugar-white sand, he claimed, stretched a quarter mile in the opposite direction from the shoreline, ending in a forest of palm trees obscuring the hotels and resorts beyond. Today, I would finally have the opportunity to confirm his memories.

After inhaling a hearty breakfast, including an overindulgence of Cuban coffee, my friends and I left the restaurant and made our way toward the beach.

Once there, we rented colorful cushioned lounge chairs, strategically placed them under one of the many thick palm groves growing out of the silky-white Varadero Beach sand, and sat comfortably in the shade—just like the other tourists on the beach that day.

We stared at the beautiful unobstructed view of the turquoise-blue ocean beyond and settled in for an afternoon of rejuvenation.

After much discussion during breakfast this morning, my friends and I arrived at the conclusion that it might be wise for us to lay off the alcohol today. It was an agreement we really sought to honor until one of the resort's bartenders unexpectedly snuck up on us underneath our most shaded spot on the beach, and asked, "Would you gentlemen care for a drink?"

George, José, and I thought about it for a second, looked at one another, and laughed.

"Of course, yes," I finally responded. "Isn't that what tourists are supposed to do?"

So much for being smart this morning. We were tourists today!

For the next hour or so, my friends and I sat under the shade of palm trees swaying to the rhythm of a constant tropical island breeze enjoying our post-breakfast daiquiri drinks. We tapped invisible bongos to the beat of the salsa music playing around us and marveled at the sight of a beach fit for a postcard.

We had not come all this way, however, just to drink Cuban daiquiris and look at a pretty beach, so I turned toward my friends and, with all the enthusiasm of my eight-year-old self, screamed, "Hey, guys, let's go in the water! It looks beautiful."

George immediately agreed, "I'm in. Let's go."

José, however, was a no-go. "You guys go ahead," he said. "I'm not feeling well. My stomach feels horrible, and my head is pounding me. I'll just stay behind and take a nap."

George and I knew better than to come between a man, his hangover, and a nap, so after careful consideration, we decided to leave José in the protective shade of our restful grove of palm trees and walked toward the water's edge to bathe in the Varadero surf.

Even though it was only May, the clear turquoise-blue water that greeted us as we walked into the ocean was unexpectedly as warm as the typical midsummer South Florida surf.

"We are in Varadero Beach, my brother!" George suddenly yelled out, opened his arms, and looked up toward the sky.

"Yes, we are," I agreed and momentarily submerged myself underneath Varadero's crystal-clear waters.

Eventually, I resurfaced for air and remained quietly in place, bonded with the cloudless blue Cuban sky above, the warm tropical sun tanning my face, and the fresh Caribbean waters caressing my skin. Rhythmic and gentle whitecap waves arched over my shoulders and unfurled in graceful cadence past me as they continued their march toward an interminable dance with the Cuban seashore beyond, sustaining an unrelenting choreography repeated here for eons. The sand beneath my feet was sugar white. I could have walked a half-mile toward the horizon and still be in warm waist-high water, and yes, the sandy beach did extend a quarter mile toward a forest of trees obscuring our five-star resort beyond.

My father was right the whole time—Varadero Beach was exactly the way he always described it.

Varadero Beach is the closest point between Cuba and the United States. Even though George and I were bathing in waters a mere ninety miles from Key West this afternoon, we might as well have been nine hundred miles away.

"George," I said, "the United States is just past the horizon. How did we allow the short distance between our countries to become so great?"

George did not respond. He did not need to. Unfortunately, we Cuban-Americans know the answer all too well. We looked at each other and nodded in silent sadness.

Incredibly Loud Condition

After bathing in the warm waters of Varadero Beach for over an hour, George and I left the ocean and headed back toward the grove of palm trees where we had left a hurting José alone earlier this morning. Wanting to check on his condition, we quietly approached his shaded lounge chair only to find him in the middle of a blissful sleep—disrupted only by the sound of his incredibly loud and incessant snoring. Curiously, no one was sitting anywhere near him.

George and I thoroughly analyzed the situation and decided that the most prudent course of action, based on our nonmedical opinion of José's condition and the terrible sounds being generated from his nostrils, was to allow him to sleep and snore-it-off.

We would instead go for a walk along the water's edge.

A Frank Conversation

George was born in the United States and grew up in South Florida. His knowledge of Cuba was limited only to personal research and his parents' recollections, descriptions, and stories of their homeland. George felt a strong bond with his Cuban heritage and had always defined himself as a Cuban-American.

Once he heard I was making arrangements to travel to Cuba, he decided to join me. He wanted to visit the land he had heard so much about, confirm his parents' memories, and discover the heritage he always felt was his. He told me he wanted to see it all through my eyes and experiences, as well as his own.

During the last five days, George and I learned that we were more alike than we previously thought. We had much to talk about during our walk this afternoon.

What was originally intended to be a leisurely stroll along the water's edge by two friends turned into a six-mile endurance trek, weaving in and out of dry and wet sand while talking about our families and lives as Cuban-Americans.

I told him how close my late father and I had been, how I had felt his presence throughout our journey, and how much I worried about what he would have thought of my return to the country he was once forced to leave.

"I wish my father could have been here with me," I told George. "I will never know if he would have understood my need to travel to Cuba in search of my forgotten memories."

"I am sure your father would have understood," George assured me.

"You would have liked my father," I said. "He had a big personality fueled by a great sense of humor. He had a way of making everyone around him feel special."

"If he were on the beach with us today," I said, "he would joke that if reincarnation were real, he would want to return as a pelican. Pelicans, he often explained, spent their days flying over the beach, eating fresh seafood, and bathing in warm ocean waters. At the end of the day, he would continue, they land on the balconies of beachfront resorts to enjoy the sunset before calling it a night and going to sleep. To my father, being a pelican seemed like a great way to spend eternity."

"Man, I'll never look at a pelican the same way again," George laughed, and we resumed our marathon walk along the Varadero Beach seashore.

Moments later, George's jovial mood turned unexpectedly serious. He stopped walking, turned to face me, and fixed his gaze on the ocean beyond.

"Mario," George said, "look behind you."

I turned around and saw the astonishing sight of a lone brown pelican floating on the water, no further than ten feet away from us, intently staring at me. I felt a cold chill flow through my body.

"Brother," George continued, "notice that there are no other pelicans around."

He was right. There were no other pelicans anywhere—not in the sky, the sand, or on the water. I stood on the shore of Varadero Beach staring at this most surreal sight and watched the lone pelican attentively and quietly until it flew away.

"Mario," George yelled, "this is unbelievable. Who are you?"

"That's what I am trying to figure out, George," I said. "That's why I came to Cuba."

Refilling the Vault

I had started the day wanting to spend it like a tourist. It was just going to be a lazy day at the beach with my friends. I did not expect any of the strange occurrences, astonishing moments, and fortuitous events that had already rewarded me with many of the memories and closures I had come to Cuba looking for to find me again today—I was wrong.

It turns out that while systematically releasing the contents from my subconscious vault this week in Cuba, I had also started to fill it up again with the guilt of returning to the country my family had so agonizingly fled from fifty-six years ago. This guilt, freshly buried, was still a consciousness too raw for me to face, stored in a place too painful to visit and guarded by a new door too heavy to open.

All week, there was not a single day I failed to think about my late father. The timing and sight of the pelican today reminded me of the special relationship my father and I always enjoyed. He loved and respected me, invariably understanding and supporting my choices. It was silly for me to question my father's approval of my need to return to the country we were once forced to leave. He would have been proud of my courage to search for my forgotten Cuban past.

Today, I did not need to summon the strength to open the heavy door of remorse guarding the guilt I had buried during my last few days in Cuba. The love and memory of my father, personified by the sighting of the lone brown pelican this afternoon, opened it for me.

I had achieved a most unexpected clarity and closure I never saw coming.

I felt free. I was at peace.

With a peaceful heart, calm demeanor, and feelings of great humility, I turned toward my still-stunned friend and asked him, "George, why are these incredible moments continually happening to me on this trip?"

He had no answer—neither did I.

George and I walked back in silence toward the beach lounge chairs underneath the thick grove of palm trees where we had left José to cope with his hangover, and incessant snoring, hours ago. Fortunately, our newly invigorated friend was on his feet and feeling much better.

A blissful sleep, it turns out, can be a great healer!

José excitedly walked toward us, waved hello, and then asked, "Where have you guys been?"

"Don't ask," George replied.

José looked at us with an unconvinced stare, curled the left side of his lip upwards, and said, "You idiots had me worried. Do you have any idea how bored I have been?"

He was right. George and I had been gone a long time, and José had no idea where we had gone or when we were coming back.

I had spent the last couple of hours discussing our experiences in Cuba this week with George and felt it was only fair to now do the same with José, so I invited both of them to visit one of the resort's several pools to cool off and talk awhile.

José walked with me toward the nearest pool. George, however, decided to go back to this room for some rest.

Once inside the pool, I grew surprised at the direction our conversation took. José's analysis of his return to Cuba was very different from the experiences George and I had this week. He told me about the feelings of anger, distrust, and bitterness he felt during our journey and how he still harbored way too much resentment toward the Cuban government and those citizens who once wronged him to ever forgive them.

José could not reconcile his painful Cuban past or find peace with his present. He was not able to enter the vault he obviously felt but simultaneously refused to acknowledge. I never knew my friend carried the weight of so much unresolved pain. I felt bad for him.

A Peaceful Night

As the sunlight waned and the day eased to an end, José and I left the pool and headed back to our rooms. Barely an hour later, freshly showered, dressed, and hungry, José, George, and I found ourselves having dinner at another of the resort's restaurants.

Luckily there was no palooka watching us eat dinner tonight—there was just good Cuban food … and friendly waitresses.

After finishing our meal, my friends and I wondered what to do the rest of the night. The conversation did not last long. Tired and sunburned, we decided to go to bed.

There would be no clubbing tonight.

Once in my room, I lay in bed lost in a place of peace, with an open heart and a mind completely at ease. Tomorrow morning, my friends and I would be heading toward José Martí International Airport in Havana to board our flight back home. My voyage of discovery to Cuba was unfortunately coming to an end. Soon, I would be back with my family and friends in the United States.

The search for the faded footprints of my Cuban childhood was almost over now. My return visit to Cuba had proven to be all I had hoped it would be and much more. Satisfied, thankful, and truly happy, I succumbed to my yawns and drifted into a peaceful sleep.

(May, 2016) The lone pelican of Varadero Beach

DAY 7

SAYING GOODBYE

Leaving Cuba

I concentrated on the last images of Havana as they whisked past the dark-tinted windows of Maidel's black Chinese sedan during our drive to José Martí International Airport this morning and reflected on the many astonishing events and serendipitous moments that continuously surprised me throughout my return to Cuba this week. Without them, I might have never been able to reclaim the lost memories of my once forgotten Cuban past.

They will always be a part of my consciousness now and continue to shape my future in ways impossible for me to predict. I hoped they'd make me a better version of myself.

I wondered if I would ever visit Cuba again. A sudden shift of the unpredictable geopolitical winds that have so often swept over the island could once again envelop this beautiful, but often forbidden, land within the historical isolationist vault it knows all too well. I dreaded the thought that the shameful iron curtain of the Florida Straits, a leftover relic from the Cold War era, might return someday to affect not just my life but those of my children and grandchildren as well.

When, I wondered, *would the political madness affecting so many Cuban and Cuban-American lives ever end?*

My friends and I arrived at the airport's departure curb, and prepared to start the process of boarding our chartered flight back to Miami—leaving Cuba once more until the day we'd meet again.

It was difficult saying goodbye to Maidel this morning. My friends and I had built a meaningful relationship with him this week and dreaded the thought of leaving our new friend behind in a country with a muddled and undefined future. I told Maidel we would stay in touch with him—after all, he was our brother now.

Just before entering through the vintage glass doors leading into José Martí International Airport's departures terminal, I turned around just in time to watch Maidel walk away.

I wondered if we would ever see him again.

What a Difference Fifty-Six Years Make

A few minutes later, standing at the rear of the interminably long queue to check in at the American Airlines counter, I found myself intently staring at the interior of the same terminal from where my parents, brother, and I once fled Cuba amid much pain and uncertainty.

Fifty-six years ago, my family and I walked into this hall and prepared to leave our loved ones, home, friends, identity, culture, and dreams behind for an unplanned and unpredictable future of exile in an unknown land. This morning, remarkably enough, I was retracing the last of my childhood footsteps in Cuba.

I had come full circle.

I couldn't help but realize how different today was. Soon I would be returning home, newly bonded with my once-forgotten Cuban childhood, at peace with myself, and invigorated to unveil the once-missing pages from my life's story, now recovered, to my family and friends.

I was not leaving Cuba in tears this morning—I was returning home with a smile.

José, George, and I successfully cleared the American Airline's preflight check-in and started walking toward the Cuban Customs Control Area. Not wanting to stand out, we walked in solemn cadence, silently detached from the hustle and bustle around us. We did not speak to anyone, and no one spoke to us.

Making Sense of a Week Filled with Fortuitous and Remarkable Moments

Making my way toward Cuban Customs Control this morning, I could not stop thinking about all the extraordinary events and serendipitous moments that continuously surprised me all week. Without them, I would have never been able to retrace the faded footsteps of my Cuban childhood, reclaim the once forgotten memories of my youth, or achieve the reconciliation, inner peace, and closures I came to Cuba looking for.

Psychologists may well define these unusual events as deep-rooted subconscious forces released by a psychological need. The faithful are likely to explain them as the mysterious power of the divine. Agnostics would possibly dismiss them as just a series of fortuitous coincidences. Others might simply say it was just good karma earned by a life of selfless deeds.

Whatever they were, I was deeply thankful and humbled by my good fortune.

Havana's Pleasant Custom's Experience

"Mario," George called out, ending my pensive mood, "get in this line. It is the shortest."

We had arrived at the Cuban Customs Control queuing area, and sure enough, George had found the shortest line. José, George, and I moved toward the orderly queue and waited for our turn to meet with the customs officer.

"I hope your stay in Cuba was memorable," the flirty female Cuban Customs agent said.

"Yes, it was," I responded with my silliest—why-am-I-grinning-at-an-olive-green-uniformed-Cuban-Customs-female-agent? — smile.

"Going back to Miami?" she asked, looking at my airline ticket. "My parents and uncles live there."

"The Cuban Diaspora," I said.

"Yes," she sighed, "the Cuban Diaspora."

After stamping my passport, she pulled her hair back, winked suggestively, and said, "Enjoy your flight."

I wished customs was this much fun in the United States.

José, George, and I left the Cuban Customs Control booths and continued walking toward our chartered flight's assigned gate.

Once there, we sat on modern perforated metal contoured seats and waited for our flight to be called for boarding. A couple of minutes later, however, an American Airlines official announced over the PA system that our flight to Miami this morning would be delayed by about an hour.

Everyone around us groaned.

With a little time to kill, I ordered a *café con leche* with buttered toast from a nearby cafeteria while George and José went looking for some last-minute souvenirs, including bottles of *Guayabitas del Pinar* for all of us to bring home.

New Friends Staying Behind

Alone and lost within my many emotions, I waited for our flight's boarding to be announced and thought about all those I had met in Cuba this week. Without them, my journey back to the country of my birth would have never been the same. I will always be grateful for their help, advice, solidarity, and acts of brotherhood.

With Cuba's future anything but certain, I wondered what would become of them in the years to come. For some, time was still their friend; for others, it was running out.

Maidel would not be joining my friends and me today. All week, he had driven, accompanied, and counseled us throughout our many experiences in Cuba. For six eventful and emotional days, we peppered one another with questions and comments. He wanted to understand and learn from our lives and experiences; we wanted to know his truth, dreams, and way of life. We met as strangers almost a week ago and said goodbye this morning as brothers.

Gilberto and Hector, the owners of my family's former Sevillano and Reparto Apolo homes, would not be coming to Miami with us either. Now in their seventies, they had nothing to gain from a life in exile. They'd prefer to live out their final days alongside family and friends in the only land they had ever known. Gilberto will continue to live in his mother's home. Hector will keep caring for a house he can now finally call his home.

Fidel Castro's son, Jorge, and his ex-wife, Ena Lydia, would not be joining us on our flight this morning as well. They will continue living in Cuba, refusing to speak to each other—victims of a love gone wrong.

My family members still living in the town of Hershey long ago chose to remain in the only place they had ever called home. Meeting them allowed me to reunite a branch of my family lost to the ravages of time and the Cuban Diaspora. My Hershey relatives will simply go on living their quiet rural life and continue the eighty-year Mateo legacy with the Hershey Railway Station—a transportation hub disappearing with every aging resident's last breath. We will stay in touch as family members do and form new memories together.

The octogenarian former sugar farmer, who once formed a part of my most rewarding memories from my childhood visits to the town of Hershey, has nothing to gain from leaving Cuba now. He will continue his life there, using his repurposed 1950s oxen-pulled sugar cart as a taxi and keeping an eye on the two cows he takes with him everywhere he goes in order to prevent his neighbors from taking them for dinner.

Oscar, my new Almendares and Sugar Kings baseball friend, will also be staying behind. He will continue to sit every afternoon on his historical and emotional bench on the *Paseo del Prado*—the only place on earth where he still feels the love of his late wife and estranged children.

Neither Pedro nor the other private entrepreneurs I met on my journey this week were coming to Miami with us this morning; they wouldn't want to. They see their future in Cuba, not the United States. I will never forget the unlimited resolve, ingenuity, and perseverance of these courageous and hopeful young Cubans as they seek to change their daily realities one private business at a time. They are the true heroes of today's Cuba and the islands' potential leaders of tomorrow. A piece of my heart will be staying behind with them, continuing to breathe Cuba's emerging oxygen of self-determination and living in solidarity with their hopes and dreams of a better future for all the Cuban people.

These new friends, as well as all others I met in Cuba this week, touched me in real and profound ways that will forever redefine me. I will miss them all.

Leaving on My Own Terms

Finally, the American Airlines flight to Miami was called for boarding. José, George, and I smiled at each other, walked out of the terminal, and started to climb up the mobile metal steps leading to our seats inside the jet's main cabin. Our journey to Cuba was coming to an end—we were returning home.

Unlike in 1960, there would be no need for my little red toy crane today—I was finally leaving Cuba on my own terms.

"Forever brothers," George said.

"Forever," José and I responded in unison.

Selfless Lessons Learned

Our chartered jet roared down the runway and soon became airborne, bringing us closer to our loved ones in the United States with every passing minute.

I thought about how even though I had traveled inside a country still under the control of the same government responsible for six decades of intolerance, economic failure, and the Cuban Diaspora, I had also found a nation hopeful for *El Cambio*'s promise to improve their daily lives and willing to extend new bridges of friendship and reconciliation over the imaginary historical canyon some still profess divides us.

All week, I basked in the warmth of the Cuban people. Their acts of goodwill, quick smiles, and offerings of brotherhood, welcomed me back with an undeniable spirit of friendship and acceptance I had not expected. That was good enough for me—I chose to forgive those who might have once wronged me and shed the preconceptions and prejudices that for too long had tormented me from inside my protective subconscious vault.

Half an hour into our flight, I looked out the airplane's window at the turquoise-blue waters of the Florida Straits below and realized that by now, we were surely no longer over Cuban territorial waters.

I thought about how, seven days ago, I started this journey to Cuba thinking only of my pain and worrying exclusively about my needs, selfishly neglecting to consider the reality and struggles of the Cubans living on the island today. My experiences in Havana this week changed all that.

I learned that Cubans on both sides of the Florida Straits lived equally anguished by the painful family separations of the

Cuban Diaspora. For every Cuban-American who once left family members behind, there is a person living in Cuba missing loved ones who fled the island.

I discovered how the daily lives of Cubans who chose to stay behind were exponentially more difficult than those of us who once made the painful decision to leave. The unabated economic struggles and lack of opportunities that have historically limited every breath of those living on the island continue to define their existence as victims of a failed and non-evolving political dogma.

Moreover, I realized that while most of us who emigrated from Cuba lived on lands with social freedoms, advancing technologies, and progressive infrastructure, those who stayed behind continually endure the ups and downs of a country forever stuck, like a broken watch, in 1959.

My journey to Cuba this week also taught me that, like me, most Cubans on the island lived with similar protective subconscious vaults sheltering them from their unpleasant memories, struggles, and painful family separation. Unlike me, however, they lived on an island historically surrounded by an invisible territorial vault encasing them within an isolated and forbidden place with no way out.

That's why, year after year, thousands of Cubans seek to immigrate abroad in order to escape their suffocating realities, claim their lives denied, reverse their stunted personal growth, and find new meaning in their existence.

A Singular Cuban Story

Cubans on both sides of the Florida Straits, I now understand, have a lot in common—we are all victims of the same failed revolution.

A Future without Protective Subconscious Vaults

I longed for a day when the dream of *El Cambio* would become a reality, improving the quality of life for Cubans everywhere and relegating all protective subconscious vaults on the island and abroad as forever unnecessary.

"Changes in Latitudes, Changes in Attitudes"
—Jimmy Buffet

The pilot announced our chartered flight's final approach to Miami International Airport. I looked out the window next to my seat and saw the beautiful and progressive coast of Miami Beach, lined by its countless modern glazed skyscrapers. My journey to Cuba had come to an end.

I was home.

I thought about how the waters of the Florida Straits, separating Cuba and the United States, had always simultaneously caressed the shores of my birth and the land I called home. Ironically, it had always been there uniting my two lives, forever defining the bookends of my one story.

Today, I was returning home, newly grounded on both shores. After all, I was and had always been a Cuban ... and an American.

Three Very Different Journeys

José, George, and I hugged one another goodbye after passing through US Customs Control. We had just completed three very different journeys of self-discovery on a trip that was a lifetime in the making.

Together, we had returned to our roots and helped one another navigate through the reality of our lives. I entered my vault and found much more than the memories, reconciliation, peace, and closures I sought. George found a vault he never knew existed within him, discovered his cultural heritage, and honored his parents in the process. José could not acknowledge his own vault and found himself unable to make peace with his past, resulting in much pain and bitterness throughout his return. Each of us was returning home after a life-changing week of our own making.

I was thankful and humbled my friends had joined me on my most emotional journey of discovery, peace, and reconciliation. We will forever be bonded by our experiences in Cuba together.

We will always be brothers.

Walking toward the American Airlines international flights arrivals area, I spotted my wife's silhouette waiting for me in the distance. It wasn't long before I recognized the face I knew so well. Her lips were smiling while her eyes tried to read mine, unsure of how to greet me. We kissed hello and hugged with a prolonged embrace. Once our eyes were finally fixed on each other, a thousand thoughts simultaneously filled our minds.

"How did it go?" Pam asked.

I looked at her, unsure of what to say, and apologetically responded, "I honestly don't know where to start. It was a remarkable week of meaningful discoveries and emotional moments I need time to digest and understand. It was a life-changing week that will forever redefine me."

"Was it all you expected it to be?" she softly asked.

"Yes, it was all I hoped it would be and much more," I continued. "My search for my long-forgotten Cuban past is over. I now know who I am."

"You look so happy," she said, still scanning my eyes for clues.

"Baby," I whispered in her ear, "I went to Cuba looking for who I was—and discovered who I am. I am finally at peace. I am free."